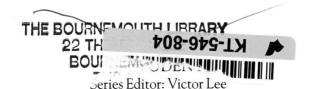

Series Editor: Victor Lee

✳

Gerard Manley Hopkins
Selected Poems

✳

Edited by Dr Peter Feeney

BOURNEMOUTH
2002
LIBRARIES OXFORD
UNIVERSITY PRESS

OXFORD
UNIVERSITY PRESS
Great Clarendon Street, Oxford OX2 6DP

Oxford University Press is a department of the University of Oxford.
It furthers the University's objective of excellence in research, scholarship,
and education by publishing worldwide in

Oxford New York

Athens Auckland Bangkok Bogotá Buenos Aires Calcutta Cape Town
Chennai Dar es Salaam Delhi Florence Hong Kong Istanbul Karachi
Kuala Lumpur Madrid Melbourne Mexico City Mumbai Nairobi
Paris São Paulo Shanghai Singapore Taipei Tokyo Toronto Warsaw

with associated companies in Berlin Ibadan

Oxford is a registered trade mark of Oxford University Press
in the UK and in certain other countries

ISBN 0 19 831961 4

Set by Pentacor PLC
Printed and bound in Hong Kong

The prose extracts quoted are drawn from the following and reprinted by
permission of OUP on behalf of the Society of Jesus: *Letters of Gerard Manley
Hopkins to Robert Bridges and correspondence of Gerard Manley Hopkins and Richard
Watson Dixon*, ed. C. C. Abbott, OUP, 1935, extracts on pp. 63, 65–6, 67, 70, 75–6,
80, 85–6, 91, 93, 94, 95, 108, 129, 135; *The Sermons and Devotional Writings of
Gerard Manley Hopkins*, ed. C. Devilin, OUP, 1959, extract on p.98; *The Journals
and Papers of Gerard Manley Hopkins*, ed. Humphry House and Graham Storey
OUP, 1959, extracts on pp. 115, 119. Some of the letters are also found in
Gerard Manley Hopkins Selected Letters, ed. Catherine Phillips, OUP, 1991.

The publishers would like to thank the following for permission to reproduce
photographs:

Bodleian Library/Lord Bridges/Society of Jesus/Oxford University Press p.147;
Clwyd County Council p.148; Hulton Deutsch Collection Ltd pp.146, 150;
The Illustrated London News Picture Library p.149.

The cover illustration is by Susan Scott

Contents

Acknowledgements

The text used for the poems in this edition is that of the Oxford Authors *Gerard Manley Hopkins* volume edited by Catherine Philips.

In preparing this selection I have had the benefit of advice and support from Dr Victor Lee and Lucy Hooper. It is right also to acknowledge a wider, less specific debt; to the many energetic and sceptical A level students I have taught, with whose interest and concerns I would hope the Notes and Approaches enter into a dialogue. For this second edition I am happy to incorporate a revised note suggested by a careful reader of the first edition, Denis Paxman.

Editors

Dr Victor Lee

Victor Lee, the series editor, read English at University College, Cardiff. He was later awarded his doctorate at the University of Oxford. He has taught at secondary and tertiary level, and is currently working at the Open University. There, he has been involved in the making of a considerable number of texts, television and radio programmes. Victor Lee's experience as an examiner is very wide: he has been a Chief Examiner in English A level for three different boards stretching over a period of twenty years.

Dr Peter Feeney

Peter Feeney read English and Theology at Clare College Cambridge, going on to complete a doctoral thesis on links between Theology and Tragedy. He retains a keen interest in the relationship between literature and religious experience. He has taught English at comprehensive schools in Leicestershire and Suffolk, further developing his interests in post-16 English through A and A/S level examining and moderating. He is currently Head of the Tertiary A level Centre at Suffolk College, Ipswich.

Foreword

Oxford Student Texts are specifically aimed at presenting poetry and drama to an audience which is studying English Literature at an advanced level. Each text is designed as an integrated whole consisting of three main parts. The poetry or the play is always placed first to stress its importance and to encourage students to enjoy it without secondary critical material of any kind. When help is needed on other occasions, the second and third parts of these texts, the Notes and the Approaches provide it.

The Notes perform two functions. First, they provide information and explain allusions. Secondly, and this is where they differ from most texts at this level, they often raise questions of central concern to the interpretation of the poem or the play being dealt with, particularly in the use of a general note placed at the beginning of the particular notes.

The third part, the Approaches section, deals with major issues of response to the particular selection of poetry or drama, as opposed to the work of the writer as a whole. One of the major aims of this part of the text is to emphasize that there is no one right answer to interpretation, but a series of approaches. Readers are given guidance as to what counts as evidence, but, in the end, left to make up their mind as to which are the most suitable interpretations, or to add their own.

To help achieve this, the Approaches section contains a number of activity-discussion sequences, although it must be stressed that these are optional. Significant issues about the poetry or the play are raised in these activities. Readers are invited to tackle these activities before proceeding to the discussion section where possible responses to the questions raised in the activities are considered. Their main function is to engage readers actively in the ideas of the text. However, these activity-discussion sequences are so arranged that, if readers wish to treat the Approaches as continuous prose and not attempt the activities, they can.

At the end of each text there is also a list of Tasks. Whereas the activity-discussion sequences are aimed at increasing understanding of the literary work itself, these tasks are intended to help explore ideas about the poetry or the play after the student has completed the reading of the work and the studying of the Notes and Approaches. These tasks are particularly helpful for coursework projects or in preparing for an examination.

Victor Lee   Series Editor

The Poems

Heaven-Haven

(a nun takes the veil)

    I have desired to go
       Where springs not fail,
To fields where flies no sharp and sided hail
      And a few lilies blow.

    And I have asked to be
      Where no storms come,
Where the green swell is in the havens dumb,
      And out of the swing of the sea.

The Habit of Perfection

Elected Silence, sing to me
And beat upon my whorlèd ear,
Pipe me to pastures still and be
The music that I care to hear.

Shape nothing, lips; be lovely-dumb:
It is the shut, the curfew sent
From there where all surrenders come
Which only makes you eloquent.

Be shellèd , eyes, with double dark
10 And find the uncreated light:
This ruck and reel which you remark
Coils, keeps, and teases simple sight.

Palate, the hutch of tasty lust,
Desire not to be rinsed with wine:
The can must be so sweet, the crust
So fresh that come in fasts divine!

Nostrils, your careless breath that spend
Upon the stir and keep of pride,
What relish shall the censers send
20 Along the sanctuary side!

O feel-of-primrose hands, O feet
That want the yield of plushy sward,
But you shall walk the golden street
And you unhouse and house the Lord.

And, Poverty, be thou the bride
And now the marriage feast begun,
And lily-coloured clothes provide
Your spouse not laboured-at nor spun.

The Wreck of the Deutschland

Dec. 6, 7 1875

to the happy memory of five Franciscan nuns, exiles by the Falck Laws, drowned between midnight and morning of December 7.

Part the first

Thou mastering me
God! giver of breath and bread;
World's strand, sway of the sea;
Lord of living and dead;
Thou hast bound bones and veins in me, fastened
me flesh,
And after it álmost únmade, what with dread,
Thy doing: and dost thou touch me afresh?
Over again I feel thy finger and find theé.

II

I did say yes
O at lightning and lashed rod;
Thou heardst me truer than tongue confess
Thy terror, O Christ, O God;
Thou knowest the walls, altar and hour and night:
The swoon of a heart that the sweep and the hurl of
thee trod
Hard down with a horror of height:
And the midriff astrain with leaning of, laced with fire of
stress.

III

The frown of his face
Before me, the hurtle of hell
Behind, where, where was a, where was a place?
20 I whirled out wings that spell
And fled with a fling of the heart to the heart of the
Host.
My heart, but you were dovewinged, I can tell,
Carrier-witted, I am bold to boast,
To flash from the flame to the flame then, tower from the
grace to the grace.

IV

I am sóft síft
In an hourglass – at the wall
Fast, but mined with a motion, a drift,
And it crowds and it combs to the fall;
I steady as a water in a well, to a poise, to a pane,
30 But roped with, always, all the way down from the
tall
Fells or flanks of the voel, a vein
Of the gospel proffer, a pressure, a principle, Christ's gift.

V

I kiss my hand
To the stars, lovely-asunder
Starlight, wafting him out of it; and
Glow, glory in thunder;
Kiss my hand to the dappled-with-damson west:
Since, though he is under the world's splendour and
wonder,
His mystery must be instressed, stressed;
40 For I greet him the days I meet him, and bless when I
understand.

VI

Not out of his bliss
Springs the stress felt
Nor first from heaven (and few know this)
Swings the stroke dealt—
Stroke and a stress that stars and storms deliver,
That guilt is hushed by, hearts are flushed by and
melt—
But it rides time like riding a river
(And here the faithful waver, the faithless fable and
miss.)

VII

It dates from day
Of his going in Galilee;
Warm-laid grave of a womb-life grey;
Manger, maiden's knee;
The dense and the driven Passion, and frightful
sweat;
Thence the discharge of it, there its swelling to be,
Though felt before, though in high flood yet—
What none would have known of it, only the heart, being
hard at bay,

VIII

Is out with it! Oh,
We lash with the best or worst
Word last! How a lush-kept plush-capped sloe
Will, mouthed to flesh-burst,
Gush!–flush the man, the being with it, sour or
sweet,
Brim, in a flash, full!–Hither then, last or first,
To hero of Calvary, Christ,'s feet—
Never ask if meaning it, wanting it, warned of it–men go.

IX

Be adored among men,
God, three-numberèd form;
Wring thy rebel, dogged in den,
     Man's malice, with wrecking and storm.
Beyond saying sweet, past telling of tongue,
70   Thou art lightning and love, I found it, a winter and
          warm;
     Father and fondler of heart thou hast wrung;
Hast thy dark descending and most art merciful then.

X

With an anvil-ding
And with fire in him forge thy will
Or rather, rather then, stealing as Spring
     Through him, melt him but master him still:
Whether át ónce, as once at a crash Paul,
Or as Austin, a lingering-out sweet skill,
     Make mercy in all of us, out of us all
80   Mastery, but be adored, but be adored King.

Part the second

XI

'Some find me a sword; some
The flange and the rail; flame,
Fang, or flood' goes Death on drum,
     And storms bugle his fame.
But wé dréam we are rooted in earth—Dust!
Flesh falls within sight of us, we, though our flower the
          same,
     Wave with the meadow, forget that there must
The sour scythe cringe, and the blear share come.

XII

On Saturday sailed from Bremen,
American-outward-bound,
Take settler and seamen, tell men with women,
Two hundred souls in the round—
O Father, not under thy feathers nor ever as guessing
The goal was a shoal, of a fourth the doom to be
drowned;
Yet díd the dark side of the bay of thy blessing
Not vault them, the million of rounds of thy mercy not reeve
even them in?

XIII

Into the snows she sweeps,
Hurling the haven behind,
The Deutschland, on Sunday; and so the sky keeps,
For the infinite air is unkind,
And the sea flint-flake, black-backed in the regular blow,
Sitting Eastnortheast, in cursed quarter, the wind;
Wiry and white-fiery and whírlwind-swivellèd
snow
Spins to the widow-making unchilding unfathering deeps.

XIV

She drove in the dark to leeward,
She struck–not a reef or a rock
But the combs of a smother of sand: night drew her
Dead to the Kentish Knock;
And she beat the bank down with her bows and the ride
of her keel;
The breakers rolled on her beam with ruinous shock;
And canvass and compass, the whorl and the wheel
Idle for ever to waft her or wind her with, these she endured.

90

100

110

7

XV

Hope had grown grey hairs,
Hope had mourning on,
Trenched with tears, carved with cares,
Hope was twelve hours gone;
And frightful a nightfall folded rueful a day
Nor rescue, only rocket and lightship, shone,
And lives at last were washing away:
120   To the shrouds they took, – they shook in the hurling and
horrible airs.

XVI

One stirred from the rigging to save
The wild woman-kind below,
With a rope's end round the man, handy and
brave—
He was pitched to his death at a blow,
For all his dreadnought breast and braids of thew:
They could tell him for hours, dandled the to and fro
Through the cobbled foam-fleece. What could he do
With the burl of the fountains of air, buck and the flood of the
wave?

XVII

They fought with God's cold—
130   And they could not and fell to the deck
(Crushed them) or water (and drowned them) or
rolled
With the sea-romp over the wreck.
Night roared, with the heart-break hearing a heart-broke
rabble,
The woman's wailing, the crying of child without
check—
Till a lioness arose breasting the babble,
A prophetess towered in the tumult, a virginal tongue told.

XVIII

Ah, touched in your bower of bone
Are you! turned for an exquisite smart,
Have you! make words break from me here all
alone,
140   Do you!–mother of being in me, heart.
O unteachably after evil, but uttering truth,
Why, tears! is it? tears; such a melting, a madrigal
start!
Never-eldering revel and river of youth,
What can it be, this glee? the good you have there of your
own?

XIX

Sister, a sister calling
A master, her master and mine!—
And the inboard seas run swirling and hawling;
The rash smart sloggering brine
Blinds her; but shé that weather sees óne thing, one;
150   Has óne fetch ín her: she rears herself to divine
Ears, and the call of the tall nun
To the men in the tops and the tackle rode over the
storm's brawling.

XX

She was first of a five and came
Of a coifèd sisterhood.
(O Deutschland, double a desperate name!
O world wide of its good!
But Gertrude, lily, and Luther, are two of a town,
Christ's lily and beast of the waste wood:
From life's dawn it is drawn down,
160 Abel is Cain's brother and breasts they have sucked the
same.)

XXI

Loathed for a love men knew in them,
Banned by the land of their birth,
Rhine refused them, Thames would ruin them;
Surf, snow, river and earth
Gnashed: but thou art above, thou Orion of light;
Thy unchancelling poising palms were weighing the
worth,
Thou martyr-master: in thý sight
Storm flakes were scroll-leaved flowers, lily showers – sweet
heaven was astrew in them.

XXII

Five! the finding and sake
And cipher of suffering Christ.
Mark, the mark is of man's make
And the word of it Sacrificed.
But he scores it in scarlet himself on his own
bespoken,
Before-time-taken, dearest prizèd and priced—
Stigma, signal, cinquefoil token
For lettering of the lamb's fleece, ruddying of the rose-flake.

XXIII

Joy fall to thee, father Francis,
Drawn to the Life that died;
With the gnarls of the nails in thee, niche of the
lance, his
Lovescape crucified
And seal of his seraph-arrival! and these thy
daughters
And five-livèd and leavèd favour and pride,
Are sisterly sealed in wild waters,
To bathe in his fall-gold mercies, to breathe in his all-fire
glances.

170

180

XXIV

Away in the loveable west,
On a pastoral forehead of Wales,
I was under a roof here, I was at rest,
And they the prey of the gales;
She to the black-about air, to the breaker, the thickly
190 Falling flakes, to the throng that catches and quails
Was calling 'O Christ, Christ, come quickly':
The cross to her she calls Christ to her, christens her wild-
worst Best.

XXV

The majesty! what did she mean?
Breathe, arch and original Breath.
Is it lóve in her of the béing as her lóver had
béen?
Breathe, body of lovely Death.
They were else-minded then, altogether, the men
Wóke thee with a *We are périshing* in the wéather of
Gennésaréth.
Or ís it that she cried for the crown then,
200 The keener to come at the comfort for feeling the
combating keen?

XXVI

For how to the heart's cheering
The down-dugged ground-hugged grey
Hovers off, the jay-blue heavens appearing
Of pied and peeled May!
Blue-beating and hoary-glow height; or night, still
higher,
With belled fire and the moth-soft Milky Way,
What by your measure is the heaven of desire,
The treasure never eyesight got, nor was ever guessed what
for the hearing?

XXVII

Nó, but it was nót these.
210   The jading and jar of the cart,
Time's tásking, it is fathers that asking for ease
Of the sodden-with-its sorrowing heart,
Not danger, electrical horror; then further it finds
The appealing of the Passion is tenderer in prayer
apart:
Other, I gather, in measure her mind's
Burden, in wind's burly and beat of endragonèd seas.

XXVIII

But how shall I . . . make me room there:
Reach me a . . . Fancy, come faster—
Strike you the sight of it? look at it loom there,
220   Thing that she . . . There then! the Master,
Ipse, the only one, Christ, King, Head:
He was to cure the extremity where he had cast her;
Do, deal, lord it with living and dead;
Let him ride, her pride, in his triumph, despatch and have
done with his doom there.

XXIX

Ah! there was a heart right!
There was single eye!
Read the unshapeable shock night
And knew the who and the why;
Wording it how but by him that present and past,
230   Heaven and earth are word of, worded by?—
The Simon Peter of a soul! to the blast
Tárpéïan-fast, but a blown beacon of light.

XXX

Jesu, heart's light,
Jesu, maid's son,
What was the feast followed the night
Thou hadst glory of this nun?—
Féast of the óne wóman withóut stáin.
For so conceivèd, so to conceive thee is done;
But here was heart-throe, birth of a brain,
240 Word, that heard and kept thee and uttered thee óutríght.

XXXI

Well, shé has thée for the pain, for the
Patience; but pity of the rest of them!
Heart, go and bleed at a bitterer vein for the
Comfortless unconfessed of them—
No not uncomforted: lovely-felicitous Providence
Fínger of a ténder of, O of a féathery délicacy, the bréast
of the
Maiden could obey so, be a bell to, ring óf it, and
Startle the poor sheep back! is the shipwrack then a harvest,
does tempest carry the grain for thee?

XXXII

I admire thee, master of the tides,
250 Of the Yore-flood, of the year's fall;
The recurb and the recovery of the gulf's sides,
The girth of it and the wharf of it and the wall;
Stanching, quenching ocean of a motionable mind;
Ground of being, and granite of it: pást áll
Grásp Gód, thróned behínd
Death with a sovereignty that heeds but hides, bodes but
abides;

XXXIII

With a mercy that outrides
The all of water, an ark
For the listener; for the lingerer with a love glides
260   Lower than death and the dark;
A vein for the visiting of the past-prayer, pent in prison,
The-last-breath penitent spirits – the uttermost mark
Our passion-plungèd giant risen,
The Christ of the Father compassionate, fetched in the storm
of his strides.

XXXIV

Now burn, new born to the world,
Double-naturèd name,
The heaven-flung, heart-fleshed, maiden-furled
Miracle-in-Mary-of-flame,
Mid-numberèd he in three of the thunder-throne!
270   Not a dooms-day dazzle in his coming nor dark as he
came;
Kind, but royally reclaiming his own;
A released shówer, let flásh to the shíre, not a líghtning of fíre
hard-húrled.

XXXV

Dame, at our door
Drówned, and among oúr shóals,
Remember us in the roads, the heaven-haven of the
reward:
Our Kíng back, Oh, upon Énglish sóuls!
Let him easter in us, be a dayspring to the dimness of us,
be a crimson-cresseted east,
More brightening her, rare-dear Britain, as his reign rolls,
Pride, rose, prince, hero of us, high-priest,
280 Our héarts' charity's héarth's fíre, our thóughts' chivalry's
thróng's Lórd.

God's Grandeur

The world is charged with the grandeur of God.
    It will flame out, like shining from shook foil;
    It gathers to a greatness, like the ooze of oil
Crushed. Why do men then now not reck his rod?
Generations have trod, have trod, have trod;
    And all is seared with trade; bleared, smeared with toil;
    And wears man's smudge and shares man's smell: the soil
Is bare now, nor can foot feel, being shod.

And, for all this, nature is never spent;
10   There lives the dearest freshness deep down things;
And though the last lights off the black West went
    Oh, morning, at the brown brink eastwards, springs—
Because the Holy Ghost over the bent
    World broods with warm breast and with ah! bright wings.

The Starlight Night

Look at the stars! look, look up at the skies!
    O look at all the fire-folk sitting in the air!
    The bright boroughs, the circle-citadels there!
Down in dim woods the diamond delves! the elves'-eyes!
The grey lawns cold where gold, where quickgold lies!
    Wind-beat whitebeam! airy abeles set on a flare!
    Flake-doves sent floating forth at a farmyard scare!—
Ah well! it is all a purchase, all is a prize.

Buy then! bid then! – What? – Prayer, patience, alms, vows.
10 Look, look: a May-mess, like on orchard boughs!
    Look! March-bloom, like on mealed-with-yellow sallows!
These are indeed the barn; withindoors house
The shocks. This piece-bright paling shuts the spouse
    Christ home, Christ and his mother and all his hallows.

'As kingfishers catch fire'

As kingfishers catch fire, dragonflies draw flame;
    As tumbled over rim in roundy wells
    Stones ring; like each tucked string tells, each hung bell's
Bow swung finds tongue to fling out broad its name;
Each mortal thing does one thing and the same:
    Deals out that being indoors each one dwells;
    Selves – goes its self; *myself* it speaks and spells,
Crying *What I do is me: for that I came.*

I say more: the just man justices;
10   Keeps grace: that keeps all his goings graces;
Acts in God's eye what in God's eye he is—
    Christ. For Christ plays in ten thousand places,
Lovely in limbs, and lovely in eyes not his
    To the Father through the features of men's faces.

Spring

Nothing is so beautiful as Spring—
    When weeds, in wheels, shoot long and lovely and lush;
    Thrush's eggs look little low heavens, and thrush
Through the echoing timber does so rinse and wring

The ear, it strikes like lightnings to hear him sing;
    The glassy peartree leaves and blooms, they brush
    The descending blue; that blue is all in a rush
With richness; the racing lambs too have fair their fling.

What is all this juice and all this joy?
10   A strain of the earth's sweet being in the beginning
In Eden garden. – Have, get before it cloy,

    Before it cloud, Christ, lord, and sour with sinning,
Innocent mind and Mayday in girl and boy,
    Most, O maid's child, thy choice and worthy the winning.

The Sea and the Skylark

On ear and ear two noises too old to end
    Trench – right, the tide that ramps against the shore;
    With a flood or a fall, low lull-off or all roar,
Frequenting there while moon shall wear and wend.

Left hand, off land, I hear the lark ascend,
    His rash-fresh re-winded new-skeinèd score
    In crisps of curl off wild winch whirl, and pour
And pelt music, till none's to spill nor spend.

How these two shame this shallow and frail town!
10   How ring right out our sordid turbid time,
Being pure! We, life's pride and cared-for crown,

    Have lost that cheer and charm of earth's past prime:
Our make and making break, are breaking, down
    To man's last dust, drain fast towards man's first slime.

In the Valley of the Elwy

I remember a house where all were good
    To me, God knows, deserving no such thing:
    Comforting smell breathed at very entering,
Fetched fresh, as I suppose, off some sweet wood.

That cordial air made those kind people a hood
    All over, as a bevy of eggs the mothering wing
    Will, or mild nights the new morsels of Spring:
Why, it séemed of coúrse; séemed of ríght it shóuld.

Lovely the woods, waters, meadows, combes, vales,
10 All the air things wear that build this world of Wales;
    Only the inmate does not correspond:

God, lover of souls, swaying considerate scales,
Complete thy creature dear O where it fails,
    Being mighty a master, being a father and fond.

The Windhover:
to Christ our Lord

I caught this morning morning's minion, king-
    dom of daylight's dauphin, dapple-dáwn-drawn Falcon, in
       his riding
Of the rólling level úndernéath him steady áir, and stríding
High there, how he rung upon the rein of a wimpling wing
In his ecstacy! then off, off forth on swing,
    As a skate's heel sweeps smooth on a bow-bend: the hurl
    and gliding
Rebuffed the big wind. My heart in hiding
Stirred for a bird,–the achieve of, the mastery of the thing!

Brute beauty and valour and act, oh, air, pride, plume, here
10   Buckle! AND the fire that breaks from thee then, a billion
Times told lovelier, more dangerous, O my chevalier!

    No wónder of it: shéer plód makes plóugh down síllion
Shine, and blue-bleak embers, ah my dear,
    Fall, gáll themsélves, and gásh góld-vermílion.

Pied Beauty

Glory be to God for dappled things—
    For skies of couple-colour as a brinded cow;
       For rose-moles all in stipple upon trout that swim;
Fresh-firecoal chestnut-falls; finches' wings;
    Landscape plotted and pieced – fold, fallow, and plough;
       And áll trades, their gear and tackle and trim.

All things counter, original, spáre, strange;
    Whatever is fickle, frecklèd (who knows how?)
       With swíft, slów; sweet, sóur; adázzle, dím;
10 He fathers-forth whose beauty is pást change:
                    Práise hím.

The Caged Skylark

As a dare-gale skylark scanted in a dull cage,
    Man's mounting spirit in his bone-house, mean house,
       dwells—
    That bird beyond the remembering hís free fells;
This in drudgery, day-labouring-out life's age.

Though aloft on turf or perch or poor low stage
    Both sing sometímes the sweetest, sweetest spells,
    Yet both droop deadly sómetimes in their cells
Or wring their barriers in bursts of fear or rage.

Not that the sweet-fowl, song-fowl, needs no rest—
10 Why, hear him, hear him babble and drop down to his nest,
    But his own nest, wild nest, no prison.

Man's spirit will be flesh-bound, when found at best,
But úncúmberèd: meadow-dówn is nót distréssed
    For a ráinbow fóoting it nor hé for his bónes rísen.

Hurrahing in Harvest

Summer ends now; now, barbarous in beauty, the stooks
    rise
Around; up above, what wind-walks! what lovely
    behaviour
Of silk-sack clouds! has wilder, wilful-wavier
Meal-drift moulded ever and melted across skies?

I wálk, I líft up, Í lift úp heart, éyes,
Down all that glory in the heavens to glean our Saviour;
And, éyes, héart, what looks, what lips yet gáve you a
Rapturous love's greeting of realer, of rounder replies?

And the azurous hung hills are his world-wielding shoulder
10   Majestic—as a stallion stalwart, very-violet-sweet!—
These things, these things were here and but the beholder
Wánting; whích two whén they ónce méet,
The heart rears wings bold and bolder
And hurls for him, O half hurls earth for him off under
    his feet.

The Loss of the Eurydice

foundered March 24 1878

The Eurydice – it concerned thee, O Lord:
Three hundred souls, O alas! on board,
    Some asleep unawakened, all un-
Warned, eleven fathoms fallen

Where she foundered! One stroke
Felled and furled them, the hearts of oak!
    And flockbells off the aerial
Downs' forefalls beat to the burial.

For did she pride her, freighted fully, on
10 Bounden bales or a hoard of bullion?—
    Precious passing measure,
Lads and men her lade and treasure.

She had come from a cruise, training seamen—
Men, boldboys soon to be men:
    Must it, worst weather,
Blast bole and bloom together?

No Atlantic squall overwrought her
Or rearing billow of the Biscay water:
    Home was hard at hand
20 And the blow bore from land.

And you were a liar, O blue March day.
Bright sun lanced fire in the heavenly bay;
    But what black Boreas wrecked her? he
Came equipped, deadly-electric,

A beetling baldbright cloud thorough England
Riding: there did storms not mingle? and
    Hailropes hustle and grind their
Heavengravel? wolfsnow, worlds of it, wind there?

Now Carisbrook keep goes under in gloom;
30   Now it overvaults Appledurcombe;
      Now near by Ventnor town
It hurls, hurls off Boniface Down.

Too proud, too proud, what a press she bore!
Royal, and all her royals wore.
      Sharp with her, shorten sail!
Too late; lost; gone with the gale.

This was that fell capsize.
As half she had righted and hoped to rise
      Death teeming in by her portholes
40   Raced down decks, round messes of mortals.

Then a lurch forward, frigate and men;
'All hands for themselves' the cry ran then;
      But she who had housed them thither
Was around them, bound them or wound them with her.

Marcus Hare, high her captain,
Kept to her – care-drowned and wrapped in
      Cheer's death, would follow
His charge through the champ-white water-in-a-wallow,

All under Channel to bury in a beach her
50   Cheeks: Right, rude of feature,
      He thought he heard say
'Her commander! and thou too, and thou this way.'

It is even seen, time's something server,
In mankind's medley a duty-swerver,
      At downright 'No or Yes?'
Doffs all, drives full for righteousness.

Sydney Fletcher, Bristol-bred,
(Low lie his mates now on watery bed)
      Takes to the seas and snows
60   As sheer down the ship goes.

Now her afterdraught gullies him too down;
Now he wrings for breath with the deathgush brown;
    Till a lifebelt and God's will
Lend him a lift from the sea-swill.

Now he shoots short up to the round air;
Now he gasps, now he gazes everywhere;
    But his eye no cliff, no coast or
Mark makes in the rivelling snowstorm.

Him, after an hour of wintry waves,
70 A schooner sights, with another, and saves,
    And he boards her in Oh! such joy
He has lost count what came next, poor boy.—

They say who saw one sea-corpse cold
He was all of lovely manly mould,
    Every inch a tar,
Of the best we boast our sailors are.

Look, foot to forelock, how all things suit! he
Is strung by duty, is strained to beauty,
    And brown-as-dawning-skinned
80 With brine and shine and whirling wind.

O his nimble finger, his gnarled grip!
Leagues, leagues of seamanship
    Slumber in these forsaken
Bones, this sinew, and will not waken.

He was but one like thousands more.
Day and night I deplore
    My people and born own nation,
Fast foundering own generation.

I might let bygones be – our curse
90 Of ruinous shrine no hand or, worse,
    Robbery's hand is busy to
Dress, hoar-hallowèd shrines unvisited;

Only the breathing temple and fleet
Life, this wildworth blown so sweet,
    These daredeaths, ay this crew, in
Unchrist, all rolled in ruin—

Deeply surely I need to deplore it,
Wondering why my master bore it,
    The riving off that race
100 So at home, time was, to his truth and grace

That a starlight-wender of ours would say
The marvellous Milk was Walsingham Way
    And one – but let be, let be:
More, more than was will yet be.—

O well wept, mother have lost son;
Wept, wife; wept, sweetheart would be one:
    Though grief yield them no good
Yet shed what tears sad truelove should.

But to Christ lord of thunder
110 Crouch; lay knee by earth low under:
    'Holiest, loveliest, bravest,
Save my hero, O Hero savest.

And the prayer thou hearst me making
Have, at the awful overtaking,
    Heard; have heard and granted
Grace that day grace was wanted.'

Not that hell knows redeeming,
But for souls sunk in seeming
    Fresh, till doomfire burn all,
120 Prayer shall fetch pity eternal.

Duns Scotus's Oxford

Towery city and branchy between towers;
Cuckoo-echoing, bell-swarmèd, lark-charmèd, rook-racked,
    river-rounded;
The dapple-eared lily below thee; that country and town did
Once encounter in, here coped and poisèd powers;

Thou hast a base and brickish skirt there, sours
That neighbour-nature thy grey beauty is grounded
Best in; graceless growth, thou has confounded
Rural rural keeping – folk, flocks, and flowers.

Yet ah! this air I gather and I release
10 He lived on; these weeds and waters, these walls are what
He haunted who of all men most sways my spirits to peace;

Of realty the rarest-veinèd unraveller; a not
Rivalled insight, be rival Italy or Greece;
Who fíred Fránce for Máry withóut spót.

Binsey Poplars

felled 1879

My aspens dear, whose airy cages quelled,
Quelled or quenched in leaves the leaping sun,
Áll félled, félled, are áll félled;
Of a fresh and following folded rank
Not spared, not one
That dandled a sandalled
Shadow that swam or sank
On meadow and river and wind-wandering weed-winding
bank.

O if we but knew what we do
10   When we delve or hew—
Hack and rack the growing green!
Since country is so tender
To tóuch, her béing só slénder,
That, like this sleek and seeing ball
But a prick will make no eye at all,
Where we, even where we mean
To mend her we end her,
When we hew or delve:
After-comers cannot guess the beauty been.
20   Ten or twelve, only ten or twelve
Strokes of havoc unselve
The sweet especial scene,
Rural scene, a rural scene,
Sweet especial rural scene.

Henry Purcell

The poet wishes well to the divine genius of Purcell and praises him that, whereas other musicians have given utterance to the moods of man's mind, he has, beyond that, uttered in notes the very make and species of man as created both in him and in all men generally

Have fáir fállen, O fáir, fáir have fállen, so déar
To me, so arch-especial a spirit as heaves in Henry Purcell,
An age is now since passed, since parted; with the reversal
Of the outward sentence low lays him, listed to a heresy,
    here.

Not mood in him nor meaning, proud fire or sacred fear,
Or love, or pity, or all that sweet notes not his might nursle:
It is the forgèd feature finds me; it is the rehearsal
Of own, of abrupt self there so thrusts on, so throngs the
    ear.

Let him oh! with his air of angels then lift me, lay me! only
    I'll
10 Have an eye to the sakes of him, quaint moonmarks, to his
    pelted plumage under
Wings: so some great stormfowl, whenever he has walked
    his while

The thunder-purple seabeach, plumèd purple-of-thunder,
If a wuthering of his palmy snow-pinions scatter a colossal
    smile
Off him, but meaning motion fans fresh our wits with
    wonder.

Peace

When will you ever, Peace, wild wooddove, shy wings shut,
Your round me roaming end, and under be my boughs?
When, when, Peace, will you, Peace? – I'll not play hypocrite

To own my heart: I yield you do come sometimes; but
That piecemeal peace is poor peace. What pure peace allows
Alarms of wars, the daunting, wars, the death of it?

O surely, reaving Peace, my Lord should leave in lieu
Some good! And so he does leave Patience exquisite,
That plumes to Peace thereafter. And when Peace here does
    house
10 He comes with work to do, he does not come to coo,
                    He comes to brood and sit.

Felix Randal

Félix Rándal the fárrier, O is he déad then? my dúty all énded,
Who have watched his mould of man, big-boned and
    hardy-handsome
Pining, pining, till time when reason rambled in it and some
Fatal four disorders, fleshed there, all contended?

Sickness broke him. Impatient, he cursed at first, but mended
Being anointed and all; though a heavenlier heart began some
Mónths éarlier, since Í had our swéet repriéve and ránsom
Téndered to him. Áh well, God rést him áll road éver he
    offénded!

This séeing the síck endéars them tó us, us tóo it endéars.
10 My tongue had taught thee comfort, touch had quenched thy
    tears,
Thy tears that touched my heart, child, Felix, poor Felix
    Randal;

How far from then forethought of, all thy more boisterous
    years,
When thou at the random grim forge, powerful amidst peers,
Didst fettle for the great grey drayhorse his bright and battering
    sandal!

Spring and Fall:

to a Young Child

Margaret, are you grieving
Over Goldengrove unleaving?
Leaves, like the things of man, you
With your fresh thoughts care for, can you?
Ah! as the heart grows older
It will come to such sights colder
By and by, nor spare a sigh
Though worlds of wanwood leafmeal lie;
And yet you *will* weep and know why.
10   Now no matter, child, the name:
Sorrow's springs are the same.
Nor mouth had, no nor mind, expressed
What héart héard of, ghóst guéssed:
It is the blight man was born for,
It is Margaret you mourn for.

Inversnaid

This dárksome búrn, hórseback brówn,
His rollrock highroad roaring down,
In coop and in comb the fleece of his foam
Flutes and low to the lake falls home.

A wíndpuff-bónnet of fáwn-fróth
Turns and twindles over the broth
Of a póol so piťchblack, féll-frówning,
It rounds and rounds Despair to drowning.

Degged with dew, dappled with dew
10   Are the groins of the braes that the brook treads through,
Wiry heathpacks, flitches of fern,
And the beadbonny ash that sits over the burn.

What would the world be, once bereft
Of wet and of wildness? Let them be left,
O let them be left, wildness and wet;
Long live the weeds and the wilderness yet.

The Leaden Echo and the Golden Echo

(Maidens'song from *St. Winefred's Well*)

The Leaden Echo —

How to keep – is there ány any, is there none such,
    nowhere known some, bow or brooch or braid or brace,
    lace, latch or catch or key to keep
Back beauty, keep it, beauty, beauty, beauty, . . . from
    vanishing away?
Ó is there no frowning of these wrinkles, rankèd wrinkles
    deep,
Down? no waving off of these most mournful messengers,
    still messengers, sad and stealing messengers of grey?—
No there's none, there's none, O no there's none,
Nor can you long be, what you now are, called fair,
Do what you may do, what, do what you may,
And wisdom is early to despair:
Be beginning; since, no, nothing can be done
10 To keep at bay
Age and age's evils, hoar hair,
Ruck and wrinkle, drooping, dying, death's worst, winding
    sheets, tombs and worms and tumbling to decay;
So be beginning, be beginning to despair.
O there's none; no no no there's none:
Be beginning to despair, to despair,
Despair, despair, despair, despair.

The Golden Echo —
Spare!
There is one, yes I have one (Hush there!);
Only not within seeing of the sun.
Not within the singeing of the strong sun,
Tall sun's tingeing, or treacherous the tainting of the
    earth's air,

Somewhere elsewhere there is ah well where! one,
One. Yes I can tell such a key, I do know such a place,
Where whatever's prizèd and passes of us, everything that's
    fresh and fast flying of us, seems to us sweet of us and
    swiftly away with, done away with, undone,
Undone, done with, soon done with, and yet dearly and
    dangerously sweet
10 Of us, the wimpledwater-dimpled, not-by-morning-
    matchèd face,
The flower of beauty, fleece of beauty, too too apt to, ah! to
    fleet,
Never fleets more, fastened with the tenderest truth
To its own best being and its loveliness of youth: it is an
    everlastingness of, O it is an all youth!
Cóme then, your ways and airs and looks, locks,
    maidengear, gallantry and gaiety and grace,
Winning ways, airs innocent, maidenmanners, sweet
    looks, loose locks, long locks, lovelocks, gaygear, going
    gallant, girlgrace—
Resign them, sign them, seal them, send them, motion
    them with breath,
And with sighs soaring, soaring sighs, deliver
Them; beauty-in-the-ghost, deliver it, early now, long
    before death
Give beauty back, beauty, beauty, beauty, back to God
    beauty's self and beauty's giver.
20 See; not a hair is, not an eyelash, not the least lash lost;
    every hair
Is, hair of the head, numbéred.
Nay, what we had lighthanded left in surly the mere mould
Will have waked and have waxed and have walked with
    the wind what while we slept,
This side, that side hurling a heavy-headed hundredfold
What while we, while we slumbered.

O then, weary then whý should we tread? O why are we so
    haggard at the heart, so care-coiled, care-killed, so
    fagged, so fashed, so cogged, so cumbered,
When the thing we freely fórfeit is kept with fonder a care,
Fonder a care kept than we could have kept it, kept
Far with fonder a care (and we, we should have lost it)
    finer, fonder
30 A care kept. – Where kept? do but tell us where kept,
    where.–
Yonder. – What high as that! We follow, now we follow. –
    Yonder, yes yonder, yonder,
Yonder.

Ribblesdale

Earth, sweet Earth, sweet landscape, with leavès throng
And louchèd low grass, heaven that dost appeal
To with no tongue to plead, no heart to feel;
That canst but only be, but dost that long—

Thou canst but be, but that thou well dost; strong
Thy plea with him who dealt, nay does now deal,
Thy lovely dale down thus and thus bids reel
Thy river, and o'er gives all to rack or wrong.

And what is Earth's eye, tongue, or heart else, where
Else, but in dear and dogged man? Ah, the heir
To his own selfbent so bound, so tied to his turn,

To thriftless reave both our rich round world bare
And none reck of world after, this bids wear
Earth brows of such care, care and dear concern.

The Blessed Virgin compared to the Air we Breathe

Wild air, world-mothering air,
Nestling me everywhere,
That each eyelash or hair
Girdles; goes home betwixt
The fleeciest, frailest-flixed
Snowflake; that's fairly mixed
With, riddles, and is rife
In every least thing's life;
This needful, never spent,
10 And nursing element;
My more than meat and drink,
My meal at every wink;
This air, which, by life's law,
My lung must draw and draw
Now but to breathe its praise,
Minds me in many ways
Of her who nót only
Gave God's infinity
Dwindled to infancy
20 Welcome in womb and breast,
Birth, milk, and all the rest
But mothers each new grace
That does now reach our race—
Mary Immaculate,
Merely a woman, yet
Whose presence, power is
Great as no goddess's
Was deemèd, dreamèd; who
This one work has to do—
30 Let all God's glory through,

God's glory which would go
Through her and from her flow
Off, and no way but so.

I say that we are wound
With mercy round and round
As if with air: the same
Is Mary, more by name.
She, wild web, wondrous robe,
Mantles the guilty globe,

40   Since God has let dispense
Her prayers his providence:
Nay, more than almoner,
The sweet alms' self is her
And men are meant to share
Her life as life does air.

If I have understood,
She holds high motherhood
Towards all our ghostly good
And plays in grace her part

50   About man's beating heart,
Laying, like air's fine flood,
The deathdance in his blood;
Yet no part but what will
Be Christ our Saviour still.
Of her flesh he took flesh:
He does take fresh and fresh,
Though much the mystery how,
Not flesh but spirit now
And makes, O marvellous!

60   New Nazareths in us,
Where she shall yet conceive
Him, morning, noon, and eve;
New Bethlems, and he born
There, evening, noon, and morn—

Bethlem or Nazareth,
Men here may draw like breath
More Christ and baffle death;
Who, born so, comes to be
New self and nobler me

70 In each one and each one
More makes, when all is done,
Both God's and Mary's Son.
      Again, look overhead
How air is azurèd;
O how! Nay do but stand
Where you can lift your hand
Skywards; rich, rich it laps
Round the four fingergaps.
Yet such a sapphire-shot,

80 Charged, steepèd sky will not
Stain light. Yea, mark you this:
It does no prejudice.
The glass-blue days are those
When every colour glows,
Each shape and shadow shows.
Blue be it: this blue heaven
The seven or seven times seven
Hued sunbeam will transmit
Perfect, not alter it.

90 Or if there does some soft,
On things aloof, aloft,
Bloom breathe, that one breath more
Earth is the fairer for.
Whereas did air not make
This bath of blue and slake
His fire, the sun would shake,
A blear and blinding ball
With blackness bound, and all

The thick stars round him roll
100 Flashing like flecks of coal,
Quartz-fret, or sparks of salt,
In grimy vasty vault.

So God was god of old:
A mother came to mould
Those limbs like ours which are
What must make our daystar
Much dearer to mankind;
Whose glory bare would blind
Or less would win man's mind.

110 Through her we may see him
Made sweeter, not made dim,
And her hand leaves his light
Sifted to suit our sight.

Be thou then, O thou dear
Mother, my atmosphere;
My happier world, wherein
To wend and meet no sin;
Above me, round me lie
Fronting my froward eye
120 With sweet and scarless sky;
Stir in my ears, speak there
Of God's love, O live air,
Of patience, penance, prayer:
World-mothering air, air wild,
Wound with thee, in thee isled,
Fold home, fast fold thy child.

'To seem the stranger'

To seem the stranger lies my lot, my life
Among strangers. Father and mother dear,
Brothers and sisters are in Christ not near
And he my peace/my parting, sword and strife.

England, whose honour O all my heart woos, wife
To my creating thought, would neither hear
Me, were I pleading, plead nor do I: I wéar-
Y of idle a being but by where wars are rife.

I am in Ireland now; now I am at a thírd
10   Remove. Not but in all removes I can
Kind love both give and get. Only what word

Wisest my heart breeds dark heaven's baffling ban
Bars or hell's spell thwarts. This to hoard unheard,
Heard unheeded, leaves me a lonely began.

'I wake and feel'

I wake and feel the fell of dark, not day.
What hours, O what black hours we have spent
This night! what sights you, heart, saw; ways you went!
And more must, in yet longer light's delay.

With witness I speak this. But where I say
Hours I mean years, mean life. And my lament
Is cries countless, cries like dead letters sent
To dearest him that lives alas! away.

I am gall, I am heartburn. God's most deep decree
10   Bitter would have me taste: my taste was me;
Bones built in me, flesh filled, blood brimmed the curse.

Selfyeast of spirit a dull dough sours. I see
The lost are like this, and their scourge to be
As I am mine, their sweating selves; but worse.

'No worst'

No worst, there is none. Pitched past pitch of grief,
More pangs will, schooled at forepangs, wilder wring.
Comforter, where, where is your comforting?
Mary, mother of us, where is your relief?
My cries heave, herds-long; huddle in a main, a chief-
Woe, wórld-sorrow; on an áge-old ánvil wínce and síng—
Then lull, then leave off. Fury had shrieked 'No ling-
Ering! Let me be fell: force I must be brief.'
O the mind, mind has mountains; cliffs of fall
10 Frightful, sheer, no-man-fathomed. Hold them cheap
May who ne'er hung there. Nor does long our small
Durance deal with that steep or deep. Here! creep,
Wretch, under a comfort serves in a whirlwind: all
Life death does end and each day dies with sleep.

To what serves Mortal Beauty?

To what serves mortal beauty – | dangerous; does set danc-
Ing blood–the O-seal-that-so | feature, flung prouder form
Than Purcell tune lets tread to? | See: it does this: keeps
    warm
Men's wit to the things that are; | to what good means –
    where a glance
Master more may than gaze, | gaze out of countenance.
Those lovely lads once, wet-fresh | windfalls of war's storm,
How then should Gregory, a father, | have gleanèd else
    from swarm-
Èd Rome? But God to a nation | dealt that day's dear
    chance.
To man, that once would worship | block or barren stone,
10 Our law says / love what are | love's worthiest, were all
    known;

World's loveliest – men's selves. Self | flashes off frame and
    face.
What do then? how meet beauty? | Merely meet it; own,
Home at heart, heaven's sweet gift; | then leave, let that
    alone.
Yea, wish that though, wish all, | God's better beauty, grace.

(Carrion Comfort)

Not, I'll not, carrion comfort, Despair, not feast on thee;
Not untwist – slack they may be – these last strands of man
In me ór, most weary, cry *I can no more*. I can;
Can something, hope, wish day come, not choose not to be.

But ah, but O thou terrible, why wouldst thou rude on me
Thy wring-earth right foot rock? lay a lionlimb against me?
    scan
With darksome devouring eyes my bruisèd bones? and fan,
O in turns of tempest, me heaped there; me frantic to avoid
    thee and flee?

Why? That my chaff might fly; my grain lie, sheer and clear.
Nay in all that toil, that coil, since (seems) I kissed the rod,
Hand rather, my heart lo! lapped strength, stole joy, would
    laugh, cheer.

Cheer whóm though? The héro whose héaven-handling
    flúng me, fóot tród
Me? or mé that fóught him? O whích one? is it eách one?
    That níght, that year
Of now done darkness I wretch lay wrestling with (my
    God!) my God.

'Patience, hard thing'

Patience, hard thing! the hard thing but to pray,
But bid for, patience is! Patience who asks
Wants war, wants wounds; weary his times, his tasks;
To do without, take tosses, and obey.

Rare patience roots in these, and, these away,
No-where. Natural heart's-ivy Patience masks
Our ruins of wrecked past purpose. There she basks
Purple eyes and seas of liquid leaves all day.

We hear our hearts grate on themselves: it kills
10 To bruise them dearer. Yet the rebellious wills
Of us wé do bid God bend to him even so.

And where is he who more and more distills
Delicious kindness? – He is patient. Patience fills
His crisp combs, and that comes those ways we know.

'My own heart'

My own heart let me more have pity on; let
Me live to my sad self hereafter kind,
Charitable; not live this tormented mind
With this tormented mind tormenting yet.

I cast for comfort I can no more get
By groping round my comfortless than blind
Eyes in their dark can day or thirst can find
Thirst's all-in-all in all a world of wet.

Soul, self; come, poor Jackself, I do advise
10 You, jaded, lét be; call off thoughts awhile
Elsewhere; leave comfort root-room; let joy size

At God knows when to God knows what; whose smile
'S not wrung, see you; unforseentimes rather – as skies
Betweenpie mountains – lights a lovely mile.

Spelt from Sibyl's Leaves

Earnest, earthless, equal, attuneable, | vaulty,
    voluminous, . . . stupendous
Evening strains to be tíme's vást, | womb-of-all, home-
    of-all, hearse-of- all night.
Her fond yellow hornlight wound to the west, | her wild
    hollow hoarlight hung to the height
Waste; her earliest stars, earlstars, | stars principal,
    overbend us,
Fíre-féaturing héaven. For éarth | her béing has
    unboúnd; her dápple is at énd, as-
Tray or aswarm, all throughther, in throngs; | self ín self
    stéepèd and páshed – qúite
Disremembering, dismembering | all now. Heart, you
    round me right
With: Óur évening is óver us; óur night | whélms,
    whélms, ánd will énd us.
Only the beakleaved boughs dragonish | damask the
    tool-smooth bleak light; black,
10 Ever so black on it. Óur tale, O óur oracle! | Lét life,
    wáned, ah lét life wínd
Off hér once skéined stained véined varíety | upon, áll
    on twó spools; párt, pen, páck
Now her áll in twó flocks, twó folds – bláck, white; |
    ríght, wrong; réckon but, réck but, mínd
But thése two; wáre of a wórld where bút these | twó tell,
    éach off the óther; of a ráck
Where, selfwrung, selfstrung, sheathe- and shelterless, |
    thoúghts agáinst thoughts ín groans grínd.

Harry Ploughman

Hard as hurdle arms, with a broth of goldish flue
Breathed round; the rack of ribs; the scooped flank; lank
Rope-over thigh; knee-nave; and barrelled shank—
      Head and foot, shouldér and shank—
By a grey eye's heed steered well, one crew, fall to;
Stand at stress. Each limb's barrowy brawn, his thew
That onewhere curded, onewhere sucked or sank—
      Soared ór sank—
Though as a beechbole firm, finds his, as at a rollcall, rank
10 And features, in flesh, what deed he each must do—
      His sinew-service where do.
He leans to it, Harry bends, look. Back, elbow, and liquid
    waist
In him, all quáil to the wallowing o'the plough. 'S cheek
    crímsons; curls
Wag or crossbridle, in a wind lifted, windlaced—
      Wind-lilylocks-laced;
Churlsgrace too, chíld of Amansstrength, how it hángs or
    hurls
Them – broad in bluff hide his frowning feet lashed!
    raced
With, along them, cragiron under and cold furls—
      With-a-fountain's shining-shot furls.

Tom's Garland:

upon the Unemployed

Tom – garlanded with squat and surly steel
Tom; then Tom's fallowbootfellow piles pick
By him and rips out rockfire homeforth – sturdy Dick;
Tom Heart-at-ease, Tom Navvy: he is all for his meal
Sure, 's bed now. Low be it: lustily he his low lot (feel
That ne'er need hunger, Tom; Tom seldom sick,
Seldomer heartsóre; that treads through, prickproof, thick
Thousands of thorns, thoughts) swings though.
    Commonweal
Little Í reck ho! lacklevel in, if all had bread:
10   What! Country is honour enough in all us – lordly head,
With heaven's lights high hung round, or, mother-ground
That mammocks, mighty foot. But nö way sped,
Nor mind nor mainstrength; gold go garlanded
With, perilous, O nó; nor yet plod safe shod sound;
               Undenizened, beyond bound
Of earth's glory, earth's ease, all; no-one, nowhere,
In wide the world's weal; rare gold, bold steel, bare
               In both; care, but share care—
This, by Despair, bred Hangdog dull; by Rage,
20   Manwolf, worse; and their packs infest the age.

That Nature is a Heraclitean Fire and of the comfort of the Resurrection

Cloud-puffball, torn tufts, tossed pillows | flaunt forth, then
    chevy on an air—
Built thoroughfare: heaven-roysterers, in gay-gangs | they
    throng; they glitter in marches.
Down roughcast, down dazzling whitewash, | wherever an
    elm arches,
Shivelights and shadowtackle in long | lashes lace, lance,
    and pair.
Delightfully the bright wind boisterous | ropes, wrestles,
    beats earth bare
Of yestertempest's creases; in pool and rutpeel parches
Squandering ooze to squeezed | dough, crust, dust; stanches,
    starches
Squadroned masks and manmarks | treadmire toil there
Footfretted in it. Million-fuelèd, | nature's bonfire burns on.
10   But quench her bonniest, dearest | to her, her clearest-
    selvèd spark
Man, how fast his firedint, | his mark on mind, is gone!
Both are in an únfathomable, all is in an enormous dark
Drowned. O pity and indig | nation! Manshape, that shone
Sheer off, disseveral, a star | death blots black out; nor mark
        Is any of him at all so stark
But vastness blurs and time | beats level. Enough! the
    Resurrection,
A heart's-clarion! Away grief's gasping, | joyless days,
    dejection.
             Across my foundering deck shone
A beacon, an eternal beam. | Flesh fade, and mortal trash
20   Fall to the residuary worm; | world's wildfire, leave but ash:
        In a flash, at a trumpet crash,

I am all at once what Christ is, | since he was what I am,
    and
This Jack, joke, poor potsherd, | patch, matchwood,
    immortal diamond,
                Is immortal diamond.

Justus quidem tu es, Domine,

si disputem tecum; verumtamen justa loquar ad te:
quare via impiorum prosperatur? etc (Jerem. xii 1)

Thou art indeed just, Lord, if I contend
With thee; but, sir, so what I plead is just.
Why do sinners' ways prosper? and why must
Disappointment all I endeavour end?

Wert thou my enemy, O thou my friend,
How wouldst thou worse, I wonder, than thou dost
Defeat, thwart me? Oh, the sots and thralls of lust
Do in spare hours more thrive than I that spend,

Sir, life upon thy cause. See, banks and brakes
10 Now, leavèd how thick! lacèd they are again
   With fretty chervil, look, and fresh wind shakes

Them; birds build – but not I build; no, but strain,
Time's eunuch, and not breed one work that wakes.
Mine, O thou lord of life, send my roots rain.

'The shepherd's brow'

The shepherd's brow, fronting forked lightning, owns
The horror and the havoc and the glory
Of it. Angels fall, they are towers, from heaven – a story
Of just, majestical, and giant groans.
But man – we, scaffold of score brittle bones;
Who breathe, from groundlong babyhood to hoary
Age gasp; whose breath is our *memento mori*—
What bass is *our* viol for tragic tones?
He! Hand to mouth he lives, and voids with shame;
10   And, blazoned in however bold the name,
Man Jack the man is, just; his mate a hussy.
And I that die these deaths, that feed this flame,
That . . . in smooth spoons spy life's masque mirrored: tame
My tempests there, my fire and fever fussy.

To R. B.

The fine delight that fathers thought; the strong
Spur, live and lancing like the blowpipe flame,
Breathes once and, quenchèd faster than it came,
Leaves yet the mind a mother of immortal song.

Nine months she then, nay years, nine years she long
Within her wears, bears, cares and combs the same:
The widow of an insight lost she lives, with aim
Now known and hand at work now never wrong.

Sweet fire the sire of muse, my soul needs this;
10   I want the one rapture of an inspiration.
O then if in my lagging lines you miss

The roll, the rise, the carol, the creation,
My winter world, that scarcely breathes that bliss
Now, yields you, with some sighs, our explanation.

Notes

Heaven-Haven

Note the subtitle (*a nun takes the veil*): to 'take the veil' is to make the vows or formal commitment a woman makes when becoming a nun. The poem is of interest on several counts: its form and idiom are very different from the style of most of the poems in this selection, and yet certain elements are highly characteristic of Hopkins. The title is an example of the kind of sound-play which distinguishes his 'voice' as a writer. The nun speaking in the text is a *persona*; an 'I' who is not the author in his or her real life, a created character speaking in the first person. Perhaps this is the nearest to spiritual self-disclosure the twenty-year-old Hopkins, still an undergraduate at Balliol College Oxford, chose to come.

> 5–8 The contrasted imagery: *sea* (8) for spiritual unrest and *havens* (7) for peace, anticipates the ambitious use of the sea as a spiritual symbol that we find in his two longest poems, *The Wreck of the Deutschland* and *The Loss of the Eurydice*.

The Habit of Perfection

Look at the title; how many different senses of the word 'habit' can you think of? How many of those senses might be relevant here?

This is another early text, with a religious context established. It shows Hopkins' interest in paradox – ideas that seem to contradict each other being sustained at the same time. Here, the idea that *Elected Silence* (1) should be *The Music that I care to hear* (4). Again, there are interesting anticipations of the concerns in his later writing; above all, the stress on the senses and the (rather pious?) belief that they are best directed to aspects of the material world linked to the divine – the taste of bread when fasting, the odour of incense on an altar.

That said, the poem displays a verbal energy that looks forward more directly than *Heaven-Haven* to the style of later poems. Phrases such as *This ruck and reel* (11) and *Palate, the hutch of tasty lust,* (13) are using sound combinations to force associations on us as readers, a key element in the stylistic repertoire of the later Hopkins. (On this, see Approaches pp. 110–11).

1 **Elected Silence** for the mystics, cultivating silence and withdrawal from the world was a pre-condition for communication with God. In a letter written about the same time as this poem (September 1866) Hopkins wrote that *silence is an excellent discipline and especially during the process of conviction.*

6 **curfew** is this meant to suggest martial law, a silence strictly imposed?

10 **uncreated light** another idea from the mystics – a spiritual light, visible only to the soul, not the physical eye.

19 **censers** vessels for burning incense in a religious ritual or ceremony.

20 **sanctuary side** part of a church containing the high altar.

21 **O feel-of-primrose hands** one feature of the mature Hopkins style is a taste for vivid-sounding, made-up compound adjectives, as here.

22 **plushy sward** a reminder of where Hopkins came from as a writer; a dead and clichéd phrase, even in the mid-1860s?

24 **unhouse and house the Lord** the tabernacle on the altar of a Catholic church 'houses' the consecrated host, the wafer of bread which believers regard as becoming the body of Christ during the sacrament of the Mass.

25 **And, Poverty ... bride** St Francis of Assisi, the medieval mystic, regarded himself as married to 'poverty'.

The Wreck of the Deutschland

As with *The Windhover,* the Notes on this poem have been kept largely to specific words or phrases. There is a discussion in the Approaches (pp. 124–31) of the poem's central relevance to Hopkins' work.

Part the first

1 **mastering** key word. Remember that the *Deutschland*'s captain was also her 'master'.

3 **strand** beach.

sway two possible senses here; motion (surge of the sea) or control (holding sway). The 'marine' references hint at the coming narrative focus in Part the second.

5 **Thou hast ... flesh** Very close to the *Book of Job*, 10, 11, an Old Testament text obsessed with the issue of human suffering and the place it occupies in a world created by a loving and strong God: *Thou hast clothed me with skin and flesh, and hast fenced me with bones and sinews.*

8 **I feel thy finger ... find** the alliterated *f* draws attention to the disturbing sense of God's power, of inescapable divine probing and enquiry.

10 **lightning and lashed rod** here symbols of divine power and (punishing) authority; *say yes* (9) underlines Hopkins' acceptance. (See the sonnets *God's Grandeur* [p. 15] and *Carrion Comfort* [p. 41] for other uses of *rod* in connection with submission to divine authority.)

15 **horror of height** Hopkins may or may not have suffered the agonies of vertigo, but it is interesting that later in his life, in a similar context evoking spiritual stress and disorientation, he also expresses his mental distress through a 'vertiginous' image. (See the sonnet '*No worst*', p. 40 [9–11]' and the Notes on pp. 84–5.)

19 **a place** of escape from the terrors described above.

20 **spell** during that time.

21 **the heart of the Host** i.e. to Christ as represented in the Host, the consecrated bread used in the communion service.

22–3 **dovewinged ... Carrier-witted** Hopkins addresses his own heart, his deepest emotional and spiritual instincts, regarding them as both peace-loving (*dovewinged*) and with a sure instinct for God, like homing pigeons (*Carrier-witted*).

24 God is present both in the terror from which Hopkins escapes and in the peace he eventually embraces – a basic theme of the poem.

26–7 like fine sand inexorably falling through an hour-glass, Hopkins describes his own condition as outwardly stable but basically escaping, disintegrating; *mined* (27) may be taken as Hopkins shorthand for 'undermined'.

28 **combs to the fall** waves can be said to *comb*, reach their high point then fall over; here is a metaphor linking water

(everpresent in Part the first) to the sand racing through the hour-glass.

29 **poise ... pane**   equilibrium; a flat, calm surface.

30 **roped with**   secured by, picking up the vertigo images of lines 14–15.

31 **voel**   Welsh term for hill (in Welsh, 'foel', pronounced 'voil'), used here for sound (alliterating with *vein*) as well as rhythm.

32 **gospel proffer**   the gospel offer or promise, i.e. the chance of redemption from sin, eternal life in Heaven, which Hopkins regards himself in line 30 as *roped with*.

33 **kiss my hand**   image of (chivalrous) courtesy and affection.

34 **lovely-asunder**   invented compound term; both lovely and separate, distinct from each other (*lovely* because separate?).

35 **him**   i.e. Christ.

37 **dappled**   compare with *Pied Beauty*, (p. 19, [1]).
   damson   a dark purple shade.

38 The key term here is *under*. Christ is part of the divine sustaining force in all of nature, but a presence implicit rather than explicit: this helps to clarify lines 39–40.

39 **His mystery**   Christ simultaneously man and God is the *mystery*, a religious truth not capable of rational explanation or analysis.
   instressed   suggests the true **inscape** of starlight and sunsets is inseparable from God.

48 **fable**   invent fictions, stories (i.e. to account for the world without acknowledging a creating God).

50 **his going in Galilee**   from the time, after his resurrection from the grave, that Christ finally ascended back to Heaven.

51 **Warm-laid ... grey**   paradox again suggesting *mystery* (see Note on line 39); more conventionally we might link *grave* (death) with *grey*, *womb-life* with *Warm*.

52 **Manger, maiden's knee**   images of Christ's birth and rearing, the *Manger* being the inn stable at Bethlehem where he was born, the *maiden's knee* belonging to Mary his mother.

53 **Passion**   the sufferings of Christ prior to his death as recorded in the gospels.

59 **sloe**   comparing the believer's spiritual experience of Christ to the powerful sensory experience of eating a ripe sloe, a wild plum with a distinctive bitter-sweet taste. The verbal technique

in lines 58–62 strongly suggests the influence of 'Cynghanedd' (see Approaches p. 110).

63 **hero of Calvary**   Christ, crucified on the hill of Calvary.

66 **three-numbered form**   in Christian theology, God is seen as three persons in one identity: God the Father, God the Son and God the Holy Spirit.

67–8 Again, as in the opening lines, Hopkins manages to suggest the context of the narrative of Part the second through the phrase *wrecking and storm*.

70 **lightning ... warm**   God as extremes; apparent contradictions; opposites (like the bitter-sweet sloe). Hence the idea of paradox: two apparently contradictory notions or ideas affirmed at the same time, extended here into lines 71–2.

73–4 **anvil-ding ... will**   one type of divine interaction with individuals expressed in images of dramatic force and heat (like a blacksmith), strongly contrasted with a gentler, more insinuating effect in lines 75–6.

77 **Paul**   St Paul, converted from a life persecuting believers by an abrupt appearance by God on the road to Damascus, recounted in *The Acts of the Apostles*, 9.

78 **Austin**   St Augustine, converted to Christianity in a far less explosive way, as described in his own *Confessions*.

80 **Mastery ... King**   note how the stressed words at the end of Part the first relate directly to power and authority, linking back to the opening phrase of Part the first (*Thou mastering me/God!* (1–2)) and re-emphasizing Hopkins' sense of the need to worship (*but be adored*) this all-powerful deity.

Part the second

82 **The flange and the rail**   (topical) reference to deaths caused through railway accidents at the time the poem was written (the 1870s); the flange is the projecting rim of the wheel which fits on the railway track.

83–4 Death personified here in military terms (*drum* and *bugle*) as the recruiting sergeant.

88 **sour**   nasty.

cringe   the scythe, traditional tool of Death the Grim Reaper, makes the meadow flowers buckle, give way.

blear share   the unseeing ploughshare; the assonantal chime (*ear/are*) is very much a feature of Hopkins' idiom.

93 **O Father**   God.
   not under thy feathers   not protected or sheltered.

94 **the doom**   the fate; there is a link with *goal* at the start of the line; both words imply a pre-ordained final target. (Compare with Notes to line 224.)

95 **the bay of thy blessing**   *bay* is an architectural term for recess.

96 **vault**   cover.
   rounds   is the difficult word in this context, but perhaps the basic sense is *rounds* as in series, cycles or as in allowance, distribution.
   reeve   fasten, attach.

98 **Hurling**   does this imply that Hopkins sees the ship as deliberately giving up the chance of safety?
   the haven   shelter, either in a harbour or from a lee shore.

104 **widow-making ... deeps**   notice the sequence of verbal adjectives here, each implying the sea as an environment actively hostile to humans.

107 **combs**   ridges on the sandbank.

108 **Dead**   meaning both 'exactly' and 'fatally'.
   Kentish Knock   sandbank near the mouth of the Thames estuary.

109 **bows ... keel**   the front of the ship; the timbers/steel plates of its underside.

110 **beam**   broadest cross-section of the ship.

111 **whorl**   propeller.

115 **Trenched with tears**   following on from the personification of an abstract term, *Hope*, in the previous two lines, does this line involve exaggerated or inflated images?

117 A line which draws attention through the blend of alliteration in the *f* and *l* sounds alongside strong internal rhymes: *fright*, *night* and *ful*, *fall*, *ful*.

120 **the shrouds**   the rigging of the ship's sails, but also as in burial shroud.

125 **dreadnought breast**   an image for a strong sailor; a dreadnought was a heavy battleship.
   braids of thew   *braids* are plaited lengths of hair; *thew* is muscle or sinew, so an image of a well-muscled character. Compare this with the appreciation of muscular build reflected in the late sonnet *Harry Ploughman* p. 44.

127 **cobbled foam-fleece**   alliterative with the *f* and *l* sounds, and

also a strongly visual metaphor; the white foam from the crashing seas resembles both wool and the massed, hard shape of street cobbles, far more familiar to Hopkins than to us.

128 **burl**   literally, a lump in a piece of cloth.

129 **God's cold**   why might describing the *cold* as God's be significant in the overall argument of the poem?

133 **Night roared**   extra impact from imagining night itself as howling, rather than those trapped on the ship?

135 **a lioness**   the tall nun whose prayer calling on Christ was mentioned in the contemporary news reports, seizes Hopkins' imagination.

136 **virginal tongue**   *virginal* due to taking a lifelong vow of chastity.

137 **bower of bone**   a *bower* is literally a dwelling place, a home – here the human body; it is characteristic of Hopkins to use vividly alliterative terms like this to present a visual, tactile image. (Compare with *bone-house* in *The Caged Skylark*, p. 19, [2]).

138 **you**   the nun? us, as his readers? Who do you think is being addressed through the dramatic exclamations at the start of this and the following two lines? Does it make sense to see this *you* as being the same as the *heart* spoken to in line 140?

141   The apparent contradiction Hopkins underlines here is fundamental to the Christian idea of human nature as a paradox: made in the image of God, so capable of perfection, but also corrupt and liable to sin, via free will.

142 **a madrigal start!**   *start* is any sudden show of feeling or emotion; *madrigal*, an elaborately composed song for several voices without instrumental accompaniment, often associated with the Elizabethan period. It may be easiest to interpret this as a synonym for the preceding word, *melting*, insinuatingly beautiful sound.

146 **master**   i.e. Christ; but the echo of 'master' as ship's captain too.

147 **hawling**   combining howling and brawling?

148 **The rash smart sloggering brine**   *brine* is the salt water of the *inboard* seas of the previous line; *rash* has direct associations with boldness, impetuosity, whilst *smart* conveys the stinging effect on the face of the salt water carried on strong winds. *Sloggering* is probably a Hopkins invention; it is up to you to decide what kind of verbal, sound associations the word contains ('slog' as in hit, thump?).

150 **one fetch**   a single, all-absorbing goal.

151 **tall nun**   it seems likely that Hopkins knew that this was also a technical term for a distinctively shaped maritime buoy. Does the pun (if you see one here) indicate macabre humour?

154 **coifed**   wearing coifs, the cap covering a nun's head.

155 **double a desperate name!**   because Germany (Deutschland) expelled the nuns and the ship has left them all exposed to the threat of a terrible death.

157 **Gertrude, lily and Luther**   St Gertrude was a Benedictine nun, a saintly mystic, pure and holy (*lily* is a Christian symbol of purity); Luther was a principal figure of the European Reformation, and for Hopkins a symbol of evil – *beast of the waste wood* in the next line. The irony is that both were closely associated with the German town of Eisleben (hence *two of a town*). As in line 141, Hopkins reflects on the co-existence of good and evil in the world.

160 For the story of Cain and Abel, see *Genesis*, 4.

163 **Rhine ... Thames**   *Rhine* as a symbol for Germany, whilst *Thames* is used in a literal sense; the ship has been wrecked on a sandbank in the Thames estuary.

165 **Gnashed**   suggesting the almost conscious violence of the elements, the metaphor implied being that of hunting dogs. (See the rest of the line and the Note on Orion.)
     Orion of light   in astronomy, Orion is a constellation named after the hunter in Greek mythology slain by the goddess Diana. As Orion was associated with stormy weather the relevance here is clear enough. If God is the hunter, and the savage elements combining to wreck the ship and drown its passengers and crew, the hunter's dogs, again we see Hopkins taking on the issue of human suffering being allowed, somehow even caused, by a loving God.

166 **unchancelling**   another example of Hopkins inventing a strong adjective; the chancel is that part of a church housing the altar and choir, so in one sense *unchancelling* means: taking (the nuns) from their religious environment (through expulsion from their German convent). But another meaning of 'chancel' is the door-screen through which nuns in enclosed orders can greet any visitors from the outside world. The nuns have been 'unchancelled' in the sense that they gain greater fame from their deaths than they would ever have expected or desired. The

two senses are complementary rather than exclusive.

167 **Thou martyr-master** i.e. God.

168 The hostile, deadly elements of the storm altered into symbols of pure beauty by God's vision in eternity.

169 **Five!** Numbers are symbolically important in many religious contexts: three the trinity, seven the deadly sins, ten the commandments, twelve the apostles and so on. *Five* is significant because it represents the wounds on the body of Christ after the crucifixion. And of course five is the number of the nuns trapped on board the *Deutschland*.

   finding emblem, special sign.

   sake that aspect of a thing which most distinguishes it besides physical shape or appearance. (See the sonnet *Henry Purcell*, p. 27, [10] and the Note on p. 76).

170 **cipher** secret symbol.

171 **Mark ... mark** the first is an imperative 'Take note!', the second the noun.

173 **scores it in scarlet** inflicts bleeding wounds.

   bespoken i.e. Christ's own sufferings are inflicted on those closest to him, most loved by him.

174 **Before-time-taken** predestined, chosen before they existed to suffer as part of the overall divine plan.

175 **Stigma, signal, cinquefoil token** the stigma is a mark that sets its bearer aside (compare with 'stigmatized'); specifically, the stigmata are the marks of the nails, lance etc. which Catholics believe certain especially holy individuals bear: e.g. St Francis of Assisi, as mentioned in lines 177–81. *Cinquefoil* describes any five-leaved decoration, while *token*, like *signal* is something that points to or stands for something else – here, the idea of Christ's suffering on behalf of mankind.

176 **the lamb's fleece** Christ as the sacrificial lamb, symbol of innocence.

   ruddying of the rose-flake as the lily is a Christian symbol of purity, so the rose is a symbol of martyrdom.

177 **father Francis** the nuns were Franciscans, members of the religious order established by St Francis of Assisi. (See link with stigmata in Notes to line 175.)

180 **Lovescape crucified** *lovescape* is probably an outward sign or show of the love in the Hopkins idiom, directly linked to **inscape**.

181 **seal of his seraph-arrival!** the fact that St Francis received the signs of the crucifixion was proof (*seal*) of his entry into Heaven. A seraph is one of the higher orders of angels.

184 Again the co-existence of opposites; *fall-gold mercies* juxtaposed with *all-fire glances*; God the merciful father, God the all-powerful judge.

185–7 **Away . . . rest** Hopkins turning abruptly to his own situation, tranquil and comfortable in St Beuno's College at the very time the nuns were in such distress at sea on the other side of the country. What is the effect on the narrative of this sudden change of scene? Does Hopkins mention his own situation as a way of heightening the anguish of the nuns, or as a way of implying his sense of guilt that they should suffer whilst he was tucked up in bed? Which seems likelier?

192 **christens her wild-worst Best** holding a crucifix to her breast, the nun makes what is apparently the worst experience of her life the best by offering up her imminent death to God as a sacrifice. To christen – whether a baby or an experience (as here) – is to admit something into the realm of God.

194 **arch and original Breath** the spirit of God that first breathed life into the creation. (See *Genesis*, 1.)

196 **body of lovely Death** i.e. Christ crucified; *lovely* because through Christ's suffering and death, mankind regained the hope of eternal life in Heaven which was lost through Adam's original sin.

197–8 **the men ... Gennésaréth** nothing directly to do with the *Deutschland*; this is a reference to the story of Christ, his disciples and the turbulent waters of the Sea of Galilee (*St Matthew's Gospel*, 8). Terrified of drowning, the disciples call upon the sleeping Christ to save them; Christ calms the waters, but not before rebuking the men for their lack of faith. The relevance to this context? Is Hopkins suggesting a comparison between the nun and the timid disciples?

199 **the crown** traditionally, the martyr's reward of eternal life in Heaven for enduring pain and death on earth for Christ's sake was symbolized as a crown.

200 The greater her distress and suffering, the more eager she becomes to gain eternal life.

203 **jay-blue** one element in a jay's plumage is a rich blue; there are several examples in his poems of the intense pleasure

Hopkins derived from experiencing the various blues of the sky. In a letter to R. W. Dixon he remarked that *crimson and pure blues seemed to me spiritual and heavenly sights fit to draw tears once.* For references to blues skies in the poems, look for instance at *The Blessed Virgin compared to the Air we Breathe* (p. 35) and the sonnet *Spring* (p. 16).

204 **pied** multi-coloured. (Compare with *Pied Beauty*, p. 19.)

206 **belled fire** is this a reference to the light of the stars, and if so, why *belled?*

moth-soft a surprisingly tactile image following on from something more visual.

208 **The ... hearing** an echo of *St Paul's First Epistle to the Corinthians*, 2; the reference is to Heaven.

209–16 This stanza is discussed in the Approaches, pp. 126–7.

217 Here the tone changes as suddenly as the rhythm itself. Why?

221 **Ipse** Latin term for He, himself (Christ); Latin because of its associations with the language of the Mass, with the Latin Bible (the Vulgate)? Or because Hopkins needs two stresses rather than one (pronounced *ip-say*)?

224 **doom** judgement or decision; often associated in Christian thinking with the Last Judgement at the end of time, the Apocalypse, when all mankind will be rewarded or punished according to their merits. (See Notes to line 94.)

226 **single eye** *single* in the sense exclusively focused on; an image of the nun's intense concentration.

227 **unshapeable shock night** compacted sense once more; the shocks experienced in the night are so traumatic they cannot be explained, made sense of, accounted for (i.e. 'shaped' in the sense of rationally ordered).

231 **The Simon Peter of a soul!** Peter here has the image of the true believer, the *rock* on which Christ said he would build his church (*St Matthew's Gospel*, 16, 18).

232 **Tarpeïan-fast** The Tarpeïan rock was a cliff outside Rome; *fast* here in the sense immovable, holding firm. St Peter was the first Pope; the Pope as spiritual head of the Catholic faith on earth lived in Rome. This is the kind of idea sequence Hopkins is suggesting here.

beacon of light at once symbolic – the Church as the (spiritual) light of the world – and concrete, *beacon* as in lighthouse beacon, apposite for a ship drifted onto treacherous sandbanks.

Notes

234 **maid's son** *maid* as in virgin; Christ as Mary's son, conceived uniquely without losing her virginity – hence Immaculate Conception and the reference in line 237 to *the one woman without stain*.

235 **feast** the ship was wrecked on the night of December 7th; the next day is the feast-day in the Catholic Church of the Immaculate Conception, so Hopkins is drawing spiritual links between the glorious end of the brave nun and the celebration of the Virgin Mary, herself a symbol for all nuns. (See the Notes to *The Blessed Virgin compared to the Air we Breathe* (pp. 81–3).

241 **she has thee for the pain** the nun has an eternal reward in Heaven for the sufferings she and her fellows have endured on board ship. Hopkins goes on to contrast her fate with that of those on board, *Comfortless unconfessed* (244).

245 **lovely-felicitous Providence** See Approaches p. 129 for comment on this phrase and its significance within the overall framework of the poem.

246 **Finger** See line 8: *Over again I feel thy finger and find thee.*

248 **poor sheep** those sailors and fellow-passengers on board the ship who may have received the grace to save them from eternal punishment through the prayers of the nun.

249 **thee** God, as discovered through nature. In this prayerful context, it may be helpful to note that *admire* can mean 'wonder at', 'be amazed by', as well as 'respect', 'look up to'.

250 **the Yore-flood** three possible senses, all appropriate in this context: the ocean; the waters of creation (*Genesis*, 1); the flood from which Noah was saved (*Genesis*, 7).

251 **The recurb** another Hopkins coinage; God's renewed control of the tides?

252 The extent of the oceans and their confining edges against land.

253 A movement to the metaphorical *ocean* of the individual's mind.

254 **Ground ... granite** stressing the believer's sense of God as the source and support of his existence, the alliterated *gr* sound used to be forceful, aggressive?

254–5 **past all/Grasp God** God who cannot, physically and intellectually, be restricted by human powers; the kind of compound adjective Hopkins invents so frequently in his verse.

256 **heeds but hides, bodes but abides** God the unseen observer, knowing everything still to occur in the course of history but let-

ting it take its preordained path; a basic aspect both of Hopkins'
own religious outlook and of the ideas sustaining this text,
characteristically channelled here through alliterated half-
rhymes.

257 **outrides**   transcends, goes beyond.

258 **ark**   here a symbol of security from (spiritual) destruction.

259 **the lingerer with a love**   Christ, whose love and mercy reaches
as far as the souls trapped in Purgatory.

261 **pent**   locked up, trapped.

266 **Double-natured name**   Christ, by nature both God and man.

267 **maiden-furled**   enclosed in the Virgin's womb; all the
descriptive phrases here and in line 268 are applied to Christ,
described cumulatively in line 269 as *Mid-numbered he*, the mid-
term of the Holy Trinity: Father, Son and Holy Spirit.

270 **dooms-day**   See Note to line 224.

272 God's intervention in the natural world through this shipwreck
has not been the kind of huge disruption of all order that will
accompany the Last Judgement; *flash to the shire* implies a more
local revelation.

273 **Dame**   Hopkins ends the poem with a stanza in the form of a
prayer to the dead nun, addressed here as *Dame*.
At our door   near us (Britons), as in just off-shore, but also
hinting at moral responsibility (why were the exiled nuns not
seeking a haven in Britain?).

275 **heaven-haven**   Hopkins used the same phrase earlier in his
career as the title of a short lyric about a nun taking the veil (see
p. 1 and related Notes p. 49); looking again at that lyric, do you
think that the verbal link is deliberate or coincidental?

277 **easter in us**   good example of Hopkins' talent for coining
powerful words, here a noun transformed to a verb. From the
context, what might 'eastering' involve?
crimson-cresseted   a cresset is a vessel used with oil or coal as a
light, often as a signal; *crimson* may simply be a colour reference
to a beautiful sunrise, itself a symbol of new life, new beginnings,
but it may also have blood/sacrificial overtones; do you consider
this would be a far-fetched reading of the phrase?

278–9 Christ as the freshly rising sun; light defeating darkness is among
the most basic of all images where natural phenomenon are used
to convey symbolic meanings (physical daylight standing for
good, night/darkness for evil and ignorance).

280 The poem ends with an extraordinary cluster of genitives, indicated by the number of apostrophes this final line contains. Why? One possible reason: this final stanza can be read as a prayer, full of longing for the return of Britain to the Catholic faith (look again at the closing stanzas of *The Loss of the Eurydice* p. 24). Two controlling nouns in the final line are *fire* (midway) and *Lord* (at the very end), the last word of the whole poem. Can you think of ways of linking these terms together, given the various processes which fire can symbolize (warmth, life, destruction, Hell, etc.)?

God's Grandeur

This poem is a sonnet, a literary form much used by Hopkins. The sonnet originated in Italian writing of the Thirteenth century, but in English literature it became a commonly used and developed form only in the Elizabethan period towards the close of the Sixteenth century. It is a form subject to rules or conventions in terms of lines, rhyme schemes adopted and structure. The majority of the poems in this selection are actually in sonnet form: fourteen lines of verse, divided in ratio 8:6, the former part called the octet, the latter the sestet. That two part structure is important; one of the conventions about sonnets is that often the sestet concludes a line of thought initiated in the octet. Hopkins uses only two rhymes throughout the octets of his sonnets; they all rhyme abba abba (you can easily test this for yourself!). There is more variety in the rhyming schemes used in the sestets, though here again only two rhymes are ever employed.

So, a poet whose preferred form is restricted to only four rhyming sounds in fourteen verses. Why? You will probably come up with your own ideas as you think further about Hopkins, but here are some opening hypotheses:

1 He enjoyed setting himself difficult technical challenges.
2 He thought that restricting rhymes helped keep expression as economical as possible.
3 He considered that a small number of rhyming sounds makes a greater impact in aural terms.

(See the discussion of this text in Approaches pp. 109–10.)

1 **charged** as with an electrical current? Implicit in the metaphor is a sense of divine creative and sustaining energy. For other uses of electrical ideas, see *The Wreck of the Deutschland*, (p. 12 [213]) and *The Loss of the Eurydice*, (p. 21, [24]), and its related Notes (p. 72) and Approaches pp. 126–7.

2 **like shining from shook foil** Hopkins' emphatic comment on this image in a letter to Robert Bridges is worth noting here:

> I mean foil in its sense of leaf or tinsel, and no other word whatever will give the effect I want. Shaken goldfoil gives off broad glares like sheet lightning and also, and this is true of nothing else, owing to its zigzag dints and creasings and network of small many cornered facets, a sort of fork lightning too.
>
> (Letter to Robert Bridges, 4 January 1883)

5 Why the three-fold repetition here? Is it effective?

6 **seared ... bleared, smeared** the internal rhyme has a rhythmical function too, continued with the rhyme (*wears . . . shares*) in line 7.

12–14 **Oh ... ah!** such interjections are the stuff of lyric poetry, features of its emotional idiom. But it is worth noting how the second sound actually dislocates a phrase, perhaps making the end of the poem thereby more interesting.

The Starlight Night

This sonnet was written at the same time as *God's Grandeur*, March 1877. Exclamations litter the text, helping convey the tone of excitement, rapture and imaginative discovery. As with *God's Grandeur*, one way of thinking about the poem is to explore the relationship between octet and sestet, the former full of romantic visions of *fire-folk* (2), *diamond delves* (4), *elves'-eyes* (4), the latter explicitly signalling Christian concerns.

4 **delves** obsolete word for 'mines'.

6 **whitebeam ... abeles** the former a tree with silvery white underleaves, the latter a white poplar.

8 **all a purchase, all is a prize** a key line in this text; as a devout Catholic, Hopkins believed that Christ's death on the cross had

saved mankind and nature from eternal damnation. The theme is fundamental to his awareness as a 'religious' poet.

10 **May-mess** fruit tree blossom, a sign of spring.

11 **mealed-with-yellow sallows!** invented compound term; pussy-willows (*sallows*) covered in a yellow, furry-textured flower.

13 **shocks** stooks or sheaves (of corn).
piece-bright paling a wooden wall through which starlight glints; a metaphor for the starry night sky.

14 **hallows** saints (as in All Hallows: All Saints' Day).

'As kingfishers catch fire'

The sestet in this sonnet is restricted to a single rhyme (just like the octet of *The Windhover* p. 18). Think about the octet, sestet relationship. Hopkins, like other poets, uses the sonnet as a device for expressing and clarifying thought. What kind of thinking is going on here?

Perhaps the crucial word in the poem is the first word of line 7: *Selves*. It is not, as you might think, a noun or prefix, as the word is characterized in most dictionaries. Instead it is a verb: 'to selve', which Hopkins coins for his own purposes, probably best paraphrased by the remainder of lines 7 and 8. You may find your feeling for this kind of reflection is developed by the sonnet *To what serves Mortal Beauty?* (p. 40).

1 The visual effect of the sun glinting off the bird and insect respectively.

3–4 **tucked** is a version of 'plucked'; Hopkins concentrates on aural experience here just as line 1 focuses on vision. The description of the bells' echoing timbre has an onomatapoeic feel to it with the succession of rhymes and half-rhymes.

12–14 A basic theme here: God loves individuals to the extent that their lives try to imitate the perfection of Christ. As the kingfisher's perfection is physical, so a man's is moral and spiritual; each is thereby part of the perfect pattern of created nature.

Spring

There is again, in this sonnet, the tonal contrast between octet and sestet to think about; the one languid, a vision of paradise itself, the other more urgent. Paradise seems momentarily captured in an idyllic spring scene, only to be qualified by the framework of sin and salvation. Paradise, then the Fall; innocence, then experience; bliss, then sin, corruption and death. It might be worth looking at the poem *Spring and Fall* (p. 30) for another expression of this perhaps idealized vision of the radiant (and temporary) innocence of youth.

3 **Thrush's ... heavens**   greeny-blue, hence *little low heavens*.
4 **echoing timber**   of the trees, the wooden roof, or both?
6 **glassy**   enamelled, shining; suggesting a perfection of form associated more with paradise than with the everyday world?
10 **strain**   offspring, but also melody, song.
12 **cloud ... and sour with sinning**   the *juice* (9) seen as a *strain of the earth's sweet being* (10), tainted by sin. Is Hopkins thinking of milk as the primal 'juice'?
14 **O maid's child**   Christ.

The Sea and the Skylark

This sonnet was written on holiday in Rhyl, North Wales, May 1877. The religious theme in the sestet is far more implicit, oblique, than in other sonnets in this selection. The timeless sound and rhythm embodied in the noises made by skylark and sea (octet) are contrasted with the *sordid turbid time* (10) of human society.

Hopkins' sensory awareness reveals itself constantly in the poems as in his prose (notebooks, journals, diaries). Here, the stress is auditory, the accent put on onomatopoeic devices to catch the contrasted sound-worlds of sea and skylark (look especially at, and listen to, lines 5–8). The following extract from a letter to Bridges written in 1882 says a good deal about this sound-world; it also gives you a flavour of the descriptive power of Hopkins the prose writer:

The lark's song, which from his height gives the impression of something falling to the earth and not vertically quite but trickingly or

wavingly, something as a skein of silk ribbed by having been
tightly wound on a narrow card ... The lark in wild glee races the
reel round, paying or dealing out and down the turns of the
skein ...

(Letter to Robert Bridges, 26 November 1882)

2 **Trench**   as elsewhere, part of Hopkins' linguistic impact comes
from his boldness in using coinages, verbal inventions. Here
Trench is a verb, not a noun, meaning 'to make a deep
impression'.

3 **With a flood or a fall**   extremes of tidal conditions, but both
words have deep theological resonances too; *flood* links to Noah
and the Ark (*Genesis*, 7), whilst *fall* echoes the myth of
mankind's expulsion from the Garden of Eden (*Genesis*, 3). Do
you think a case might be made for this biblical aspect to the
phrase as used here by Hopkins, particularly in the light of the
ideas developed in the sestet? Or are any biblical echoes merely
a coincidence?

9 **this shallow and frail town**   Rhyl? The resort, located a few
miles to the north of St Beuno's College, on the North Wales
coast, was largely a by-product of the building of the Chester to
Holyhead railway in the 1840s. It was a favourite haunt for
holidaymakers from the industrial towns of nearby Lancashire.

10 **turbid**   muddy, crowded.

12 **earth's past prime**   another Garden of Eden allusion?

In the Valley of the Elwy

This is a curious sonnet because it seems to run counter to the
tendency highlighted elsewhere for Hopkins's octets to establish a
'naturalist' context into which explicitly Christian motifs are
introduced in the sestet. Here, the octet refers to the poet's happy
memories of hospitality when he thought he did not deserve it. The
start of the sestet probably leads you on to assume that this
welcoming house was in Wales, in that very valley of the Elwy from
which the sonnet gets its title. So lines 9–10 might be read as linking
a hospitable Welsh home to the welcoming natural environment of
Wales itself. But if this is so neatly the case, where does line 11 fit in?

On this reading of the poem, isn't the *inmate* the kindly host who cared for the poet? Further mystification, with the outline of a possible solution, comes in a letter to Bridges where Hopkins writes:

> The kind people of the sonnet were the Watsons of Shooter's Hill, London, nothing to do with the Elwy ... The frame of the sonnet is a rule of three sum wrong, thus: As the sweet smell to those kind people so the Welsh landscape is NOT to the Welsh; and then the author and principle of all four terms is asked to bring the sum right.
> (Letter to Robert Bridges, 8 April 1879)

This sonnet offers a valuable lesson about premature conclusions reached from misleading contextual clues! It also amply demonstrates the quirky, contrary nature of Hopkins' intellect – always ready to go off at a tangent or turn an expected line of thought inside out. You have been warned.

5   **cordial**   literally, something stimulating the heart – so, refreshing, warm, welcoming.
    made those kind people a hood   the air 'hoods' (covers and protects) the people.
9   **combes**   gentle valleys.
12–14   As in *The Sea and the Skylark* (p. 17), do we see Hopkins' sense of the imperfect and evil state of mankind in nature breaking through?

The Windhover

You may find it helpful to refer to the discussion of this poem in *Approaches* (pp. 102–5). The textual notes here are intended to complement that discussion.

1   **morning's minion**   a *minion* is, literally, a favourite child or servant, a king's favourite; the French origins of the word (*mignon* meaning darling) link directly to *daylight's dauphin* (2).
2   **daylight's dauphin**   crown prince, heir to daylight.
    dapple-dawn-drawn   attracted from his overnight resting place by the light of dawn. Note the use of compounds for both economy and impact.

4 **wimpling**   rippling, through effort and through effect of wind?

6 **bow-bend**   wide arc.

8 **achieve**   achievement; noun disguised as verb again, for economy and impact?

9 **plume**   note the proximity in the line to *pride*; peacock and ostrich plumes are often associated with (human) display, or do you think it more likely that Hopkins is still restricting his thought to the falcon's own feathers?

10 **Buckle!**   crucial (and ambiguous) term; collapse, link together, put on armour, give way to – all possible senses, none obviously ruled out by this context. It is the imperative, (commanding) verb which controls the whole of the previous line.

11 **chevalier**   knight, hero; like *minion* (1) and *dauphin* (2), a word taken directly from French, and again the medieval, chivalric colouring.

12 **sillion**   strip of land to be ploughed.

13 **blue-bleak**   *bleak* because, apparently, lifeless and cold?

14 **gall**   literally, injure, annoy or humiliate themselves; how can embers be described as doing things they feel, physically or emotionally, unless it is not just embers that these lines are concerned with?

gash gold-vermilion   are cut open to reveal rich colours (contrasted with *blue-bleak* [13]), associated with the colours of royalty in heraldry. *Vermilion* may also have associations with the colour of blood. Some commentators have suggested that just as the start of the poem is set at dawn, so the image at the close is of dusk; how persuasive do you find this reading yourself?

Pied Beauty

Structurally, this poem is a curiosity. It is a 'curtal' sonnet, condensed or abbreviated into 10½ lines rather than the usual 14. The initial octet is now a sestet and the closing sestet is now a quartet, with a final half-line or tailpiece. (See also *Peace* p. 28).

In celebrating the heterogeneous, prolific character of the natural world, the poem has often been regarded as displaying Hopkins' voice and technique at their most characteristic. Why do you think editors of anthologies have so frequently preferred this poem against others in giving readers a sense of Hopkins' writing? For further discussion of this poem see Approaches pp. 109–10.

The word *Pied* in the title means 'Parti-coloured ... also of three or more colours in patches or blotches' (*OED*).

2 **of couple-colour as a brinded cow**   variously coloured, like a 'brindled' cow.

4 **Fresh-firecoal chestnut-falls**   *Chestnuts as bright as coals or spots of vermilion*, an observation Hopkins made in his Journal (in September 1868) nearly a decade before writing this sonnet.

5 **fold, fallow, and plough**   referring respectively to grazing, fallow and cultivated fields; 'mixed' farming giving the landscape the patchwork effect Hopkins notes and admires.

6 **trim**   dress, clothing.

7 **counter ... spare**   unique ... undecorated.

8 **freckled**   variegated.

10 **beauty past change**   the eternal, so immutable, beauty of the creator contrasted with the ever-changing variety evident in nature, the creation.

The Caged Skylark

This sonnet has a rather conventional premise: the wild bird trapped in a cage, a symbol for the eternal soul trapped in a mortal body. It is not, perhaps, made more interesting by any sense of the poet going off at tangents? Wild bird in cage: soul in body is an analogy, an extended comparison. Does Hopkins manage to sustain that analogy throughout the length of his sonnet or do you feel that instead the comparison breaks down before the end?

1 **scanted**   typically fertile invention; the sense something like 'existing in a mean and basic way'.

2 **bone-house**   rib-cage, body.

3 **fells**   moors.

12–14   an allusion to the Christian belief that the virtuous souls in Heaven will reassume their physical form after the Last Judgement.

Hurrahing in Harvest

This sonnet reveals an ecstatic awareness of nature enhanced and intensified by awareness of the divine being who creates and sustains. Hopkins describes it, in a letter to Bridges of July 1878, as: *the outcome of half an hour of extreme enthusiasm as I walked home alone one day from fishing in the Elwy*. The emphatic alliterations of lines 1–4 certainly evoke something at once sensuous and intoxicated (*extreme enthusiasm?*).

  1 **barbarous**   wild
  6 **glean**   a pun; 'gleaning' is part of the cleaning up process after the harvest and also a word for 'glimpsing'.
11–12 These lines form the religious nucleus of this text; physical, inanimate nature is informed by the divine, the poet's joy in nature's beauty is virtually interchangeable with his joy at being in the presence of God.
 13 **The heart rears wings**   a complex image. Do you think here of the windhover, of the Holy Spirit symbolized as the dove of peace? Is the sense less prescriptive or specific than either of these?

The Loss of the Eurydice

A shorter sea narrative than *The Wreck of the Deutschland*, but again a text in which Hopkins tries to integrate elements of dramatic narrative and religious reflection.

Hopkins took the 'musical' dimensions of this text – its aural impact when read aloud correctly – very seriously, as this remark in a letter to Bridges indicates:

> To do the *Eurydice* any kind of justice you must not slovenly read it with the eyes but with your ears, as if the paper were declaiming it at you. For instance the line 'she had come from a cruise, training seamen' read without proper stress and declaim is mere Lloyd's Shipping Intelligence; properly read it is quite a different thing. Stress is the life of it.   (Letter to Robert Bridges, 13 May 1878)

This concern for the musical aspect, the effect on us as listeners rather than readers, often figures in Hopkins' written comments on his work (See for example the Notes to the later sonnets *Harry Ploughman* (pp. 92–3) and *Tom's Garland* (pp. 93–5), and Approaches pp. 112–14.)

Some historical details may help to establish the context of Hopkins' narrative. The *Eurydice* was a naval training ship which foundered off the Isle of Wight in March 1878 as it returned from a voyage to the West Indies. Unlike the *Deutschland*, there were no persecuted German nuns on board to provoke Hopkins' sense of awe and outrage, but the text does suggest that he was inspired by the loss of so many young sailors to create this dramatic reflection on life and death.

The poem falls into two fairly distinct parts. Stanzas 1–21 focus largely on the events leading up to and surrounding the capsize of the ship in a severe storm. The captain, Marcus Hare, is singled out, as is one Sydney Fletcher, who through *a lifebelt and God's will* (63) survived the sinking and was rescued by another vessel. The final three stanzas of this first part focus quite explicitly on the corpse of a young sailor, *of lovely manly mould* (74), and on Hopkins' sense of loss at his beauty and talent wasted.

By contrast, stanzas 22–30, like the final section of *The Wreck of the Deutschland*, shift attention from the watery drama to attempt a link between a local tragedy and a national, historical one. Your own thoughts about the success or otherwise of the poem may well hinge on whether you find this imaginative leap convincing. Hopkins is thinking back to the pre-Reformation era when Roman Catholicism was the mode of Christianity practised in Britain. For Hopkins, the devout convert and Jesuit priest, this was the only authentic and true form of Christian witness. He is reflecting on the fact that those who drowned in the *Eurydice* died unabsolved, that is not in a state of grace before God.

As in the longer poem, many of the challenges Hopkins sets us as readers are caused by his compressed idiom; it is up to you to decide whether the effort of wrestling with those challenges is finally justified.

1 **concerned thee** ambiguous? meaning 'mattered to you' or 'was your responsibility'; significant this early in the poem.

5–6 **One … oak!** a dramatic pun; *hearts of oak* equals sailors, cut down like a mighty oak by a powerful lightning bolt.

7 **flockbells** a Hopkins coinage; the bells on sheep grazing on the steep seaward facing slopes (*forefalls* (8) another invention).

12 **lade** a contraction rather than an invention; more expected would be 'lading' meaning 'cargo'.

16 **bole and bloom** a nicely alliterative phrase, trunk and foliage, the whole tree.

23 **Boreas** north wind (from Greek mythology).

24 **deadly-electric** vivid, curiously modern-sounding phrase, referring to the lightning storm. Readers have found the intended rhyme in lines 23–4 (*he/Came … electric*, the hard C of *Came* rhyming with the *ic* of *electric*) very perverse and forced; what is your view?

27–8 **Hailropes … Heavengravel** from the perverse to the inspired? Aggressive sounding coinages for foul weather.

29–32 **Carisbrook … Appledurcombe … Ventnor … Boniface Down** places on the Isle of Wight, familiar to Hopkins from holidays.

34 **royals** sails used in fine weather. Is there the hint of something reckless about the conduct of the ship as it is about to meet severe weather?

40 **messes of mortals** alliteration plus a pun ('mess' as in ship's mess; also as in untidy heap, or even human excrement, waste?).

43 **she** the ship; what had protected the men from the sea is now their tomb.

47 **Cheer's death** despair.

48 **champ-white** why *champ*?

50 **Right, rude of feature …** paraphrase as 'Right – duty, the voice of conscience – is thought to say to the captain …'

53–6 Is this stanza made opaque in meaning by fussy syntax? It isn't helped by the feeling that the actual thought here, paraphrased by Hopkins in a letter to Bridges in May 1878 as: *even those who seem unconscientious will act the right part at a great push*, seems at a tangent to the direction of the narrative.

68 **rivelling** causing to wrinkle.

77 **how all things suit!** beauty as the absolute symmetry or agreement of constituent parts. This idea is very important to

Hopkins, and the essence of his own aesthetic throughout his poetry. (See Approaches pp. 118–20).

85 **He was but one ... more** the transition point to the wider historical reflection developed in the final nine stanzas.

89 **bygones** the Reformation, the dissolution of the monasteries etc. in the Sixteenth century, when Henry VIII broke the links between the Christian faith in England and the traditional authority of the Pope in Rome.

92 **hoar-hallowed shrines unvisited** shrines, places of pilgrimage, made holy through their very age (*hoar*). Note the richness of the vowel sounds here.

94 **wildworth** wild flowers; a metaphor for the sailors, now *blown*.

95–6 **in/Unchrist** a striking phrase; the sailors are damned because they were raised in a country (Britain) Hopkins sees as having turned its back on God (*all rolled in ruin*).

98 **Wondering ... it** this opens up a huge theological speculation; if the Reformation was so complete a tragedy for the British people, why did God allow it to happen?

101 **a starlight-wender** A nocturnal traveller, a medieval pilgrim, guided by the stars towards the shrine which is the goal of his journey.

102 **Walsingham Way** the pilgrims' way to Walsingham, the north Norfolk shrine to the Virgin Mary.

117–20 **Not that hell ... pity-eternal** It might be worth thinking about the tone or tones with which this poem ends and comparing them with the ending of *The Wreck of the Deutschland*. The thought here is part of Catholic eschatology as Hopkins understood it: the Catholic doctrine of salvation. Until the Last Judgement itself, the fate of those who die outside the state of grace will remain undecided; this should encourage their relatives and loved ones to continue praying for their salvation as divine pity may yet be stirred.

Duns Scotus's Oxford

The Duns Scotus of this sonnet was a medieval Catholic philosopher, a vital formative influence on the mind of Hopkins after his conversion to Catholicism. The basics of that influence are looked at in the Approaches (p. 119). He is supposed to have lectured in

Oxford sometime at the start of the Fourteenth century. The sonnet can be viewed as a well-crafted piece of intellectual and spiritual hero-worship: *this air I gather and I release/He lived on*; (9–10).

The octet provides Hopkins with the chance to create a description of the Oxford he himself knew well. It also allows him to attack the (sub)urban sprawl of the expanding city of the 1870s, the *graceless growth* (7) interposing itself between the ancient collegiate centre and the beauties of the surrounding countryside.

 4 **coped** matched (their power).

 5 **sours** Hopkins notes in a letter of February 1879, *that landscape, the charm of Oxford, green shouldering grey, which is already abridged and soured.*

 12 **realty** realism. The phrase used here underlines Hopkins' admiration for Duns Scotus as a metaphysician, a philosopher interested in the nature of existence and being itself.

 14 The reference here is to a famous theological debate in Paris, where Hopkins' hero successfully defended the doctrine of the Immaculate Conception, the belief that Mary the mother of Christ was the only human to be born without the stain of original sin (*without spot*). The doctrine was an article of Catholic faith in which Hopkins had a fierce belief.

Binsey Poplars

A lyric constructed in three eight-line stanzas. The feeling informing the text seems distinctly contemporary. Can you find any other evidence in this selection of Hopkins' 'green' credentials? For further discussion of this poem see Approaches pp. 114–15.

 1 **aspens** broad-leaved poplars.

 10 **delve or hew** dig or chop down.

 12–15 A dramatic image; nature's integrity vulnerable as eyesight itself.

 19 **After-comers** posterity; but an obsolete term, deliberately revived here by Hopkins. Why?

 21 **unselve** Disintegration/destruction of the scene's unique, particular identity. (On *Selves*, see Notes to line 7 of '*As kingfishers catch fire*' [p. 64]).

 22–4 The repetition is curious, as if Hopkins wishes to stress the pathos of the destruction by repeating this tender-sounding phrase. The word *especial* has particular force in Hopkins' mind; it is associated with 'selve' and **inscape** (see Approaches, pp. 118–19) as a term referring to the unique and unrepeatable quality in our experience of phenomena. See also line 2 of *Henry Purcell* (p. 27), probably written at about the same time, during Hopkins' short period of parish work in Oxford. Another possible explanation of the marked repetitions at the end of this text is that Hopkins may have been thinking of a musical setting for the poem. None of these explanations excludes the others.

Henry Purcell

Henry Purcell (1659–95) is generally regarded as the greatest English composer of the Seventeenth century. The veneration felt by Hopkins is doubly evident here, with the prose dedication to Purcell's *divine genius* prefacing the sonnet itself.

It is only fair to add that whereas Hopkins' feeling for the philosopher, Duns Scotus, is expressed in a comparatively direct manner, the initial impression any reader will have of the Purcell sonnet is of a tortuous, cryptic puzzle. Part of the challenge comes from the (simple) fact that Hopkins saw the sonnet in general as a vehicle for thought; complex thoughts conveyed within the restrictive terms of a sonnet are likely to emerge looking even more complex. This compacting tendency gets more pronounced in Hopkins' later sonnets, but is just as much a feature here.

Some indication of the problem is offered by the paraphrase of the sonnet which Hopkins provided in a letter to Bridges of January 1883; it is worth quoting, not only for the light it may shed on this sonnet, but also as an example of the clarity which often distinguishes Hopkins' prose. Additionally, the fact that Hopkins realized, to his dismay, that even his most ardent readers found barriers to understanding may give you comfort in your own engagements with these poems!

> The sonnet on Purcell means this: 1–4. I hope Purcell is not damned for being a Protestant, because I love his genius. 5–8. And that not so much for gifts he shares, even though it shd. be in higher measure, with other musicians as for his own individuality. 9–14. So

that while he is aiming only at impressing me his hearer with the meaning in hand I am looking out meanwhile for his specific, his individual markings and mottlings, 'the sakes of him'. It is as when a bird thinking only of soaring spreads its wings: a beholder may happen then to have his attention drawn by the act to the plumage displayed. In particular, the first lines mean: May Purcell, O may he have died a good death and that soul which I love so much and which breathes or stirs so unmistakeably in his works have parted from the body and passed away ... It is somewhat dismaying to find I am so unintelligible though, especially in one of my very best pieces.

(Letter to Robert Bridges, 4 January 1883)

6 **nursle**   foster, care for.
8 **self**   key term; when he listens to Purcell's music, Hopkins experiences his **inscape**, the unique and particular identity which distinguishes Purcell and his genius from all other men (and all other geniuses).
9 **lift me, lay me!**   a kind of hopeful prayer; may the angelic music inspire and/or soothe me!
10 **sakes**   In the same letter to Bridges as quoted above, Hopkins remarks, *'Sakes' is hazardous: about that point I was more bent on saying my say than on being understood in it.* In any consideration of Hopkins' difficulty, that remark is worth recalling; comprehension in a reader is seen as secondary to precise expression of an image or perception. For Hopkins, a thing's 'sake' is that which most distinguishes it outside its physical form, so for a human genius, the 'sake' would be that aspect of genius for which the individual is celebrated, so for Purcell, his music.
    quaint moonmarks   *I was thinking of a bird's quill feathers*, Hopkins remarks in same letter as above.
13 **wuthering**   noise and rush of wind. (Compare with *Wuthering Heights*.)
14 **but**   only, merely.

Peace

Like *Pied Beauty* (p. 19), this is a 'curtal' sonnet. Note how the rhyme scheme links together the two structures of the sonnet. Rhythmically, the use of repetitions and the series of rhetorical questions addressed to Peace give the first part of the poem a restless, even nervous quality. The effect, by design, is anything but peaceful! This dissonance between style and subject matter may offer a useful starting point for discussion of the text.

> 7 **reaving**   robbing, plundering.
> 9 **plumes to Peace thereafter**   *plumes* continues the bird metaphor set up in the opening six lines; the sense is of a fledgling (*Patience* [8]) maturing into the splendour of the adult bird (Peace itself).

Felix Randal

In this sonnet links between life and poetry seem especially intimate; a poem arising directly from Hopkins' experience of life and death amongst the working-class poor of Liverpool as a parish priest.

On one level, this is a poem about the death of a once strong and healthy man, a man dependent on physical strength in his working life, and the way that death appears to the priest who had comforted him in his final illness. But alongside that narrative other elements appear: Hopkins' acute sense of physical beauty and prowess; the relationship between physical distress and spiritual relief; the strong feeling of mortality emerging at the close of the poem. One way into this text is to think about it as an elegy: a poem of mourning for the dead, for a fellow man whose **inscape** Hopkins admired for very different reasons to the inscapes celebrated in his sonnets on Henry Purcell and Duns Scotus.

> 1 **farrier**   person working in a smithy making and fitting horse-shoes.
> **O is he dead then?**   why do you think Hopkins uses the present tense question form here?
> 6 **anointed**   given the last rites, a sacrament reserved for those gravely ill or close to death.

7 **sweet reprieve and ransom** Holy Communion; the re-enactment of the sacrifice through which Christ on the cross reconciled God and man.

8 **all road ever** Lancashire dialect form for 'however' used deliberately in a Lancashire context: the farrier was a member of Hopkins' Liverpool parish.

13 **random** (architecture) composed of rough, irregular stones.
grim grimy (dialect).

14 **sandal!** archaic term for type of horseshoe, rather than a convenient rhyme for *Randal!* It is worth noting here that the farrier's surname is a pseudonym, the actual name was Spencer, but the forename is identical. *Felix* is a Latin word, meaning 'lucky' or 'fortunate'; appropriate or ironic in the case of the farrier of Hopkins' sonnet?

Spring and Fall

Notice the dedication, *to a Young Child*, the *Margaret* addressed right from the start of the opening line. If you have a strong feeling for this poem, the factors behind that feeling may be as follows: the directness of form, the easy fluency of the rhythm and the accessibility of images and language serve to heighten the feeling that Hopkins is dealing with a great theme here, all too glibly summarized by a term like 'innocence and experience'. How do you react to the thought that the poem has a direct appeal missing from at least some of the sonnets with their precise and complex lines of argument? For further discussion of this poem see Approaches pp. 117–18.

2 **unleaving** a neat invention; what trees do in the autumn.

8 **worlds of wanwood leafmeal lie** the alliteration helps stress an evocative image, which risks being shattered if analysed too literally. The young girl is upset (*grieving* [1]), by the first signs of autumn in a wood; her older, more experienced self will have so many other elements of transience or mutability to grieve over that she will not be touched again by autumn and its changes, even on the grandest scale.

13 **ghost** soul, spirit.

14 **blight** of original sin?

Inversnaid

Three stanzas of intense verbal description, followed by a flat, generalized conclusion; a fair response to the poem, or do you think there is more to the relationship between the parts than this suggests? For further discussion see Approaches p. 116.

3   **coop ... comb**   water enclosed (as in a rock pool); water freely moving.

4   **Flutes**   architectural expression for 'ridges', applied here not to stonework but to water channelled between rocks by a strong current.

6   **twindles**   Lancashire dialect word for 'twins', but also perhaps a Hopkins invention, combining 'twins' and 'spindles'?

9   **Degged**   Lancashire term again meaning 'sprinkled'. (See *Felix Randal* p. 29 [8] for other use of Lancashire dialect.)

11   **heathpacks**   heather.
     flitches of fern   like thin cuts from a tree trunk.

12   **beadbonny ash**   mountain ash, full of autumn berries (an apt use of the Scots *bonny* here, for the Scottish context).

The Leaden Echo and the Golden Echo

Some background information might be helpful here. Hopkins first came across the legend of St Winefred whilst studying for the Catholic priesthood at St Beuno's College in North Wales. He was attracted to the legend and to the well at Holywell named after the saint. He planned a verse drama on the legend, but although some fragments (such as this song) were written, he never completed the project. The legend itself is about chastity and martyrdom, religious concepts with which Hopkins is often preoccupied. Winefred, daughter of a Seventh century Welsh lord and niece of St Beuno, decides to dedicate her virginity to God. Prince Caradoc becomes obsessed by her beauty; she spurns him and enraged by such rejection he cuts off her head with his sword. A well springs up where the head falls to the ground. In some versions St Beuno brings his niece back to life and his curse then dispatches Caradoc to damnation.

It makes sense to assume that Hopkins composed this 'Maidens' song' with a musical setting in mind, and with two contrasted voices or voice groups, the one 'leaden', the other 'golden'. All of this suggests an antiphonal setting, with the contrasts in mood in the two echoes underlined by a musical treatment exploiting the opportunities the text offers for word-painting and dramatic oppositions. For further discussion of this poem see Approaches pp.120–1.

Leaden Echo

1 Hopkins' remarks on this beginning, in a letter to Bridges of November 1882, throw considerable light on what kind of effects and mood he was trying to establish in this poem:

> I cannot satisfy myself about the first line. You must know that words like 'charm' and 'enchantment' will not do: the thought is of beauty as something that can be physically kept and lost and by physical things only, like keys: then the things must come from the 'mundus muliebris' [the world of women]; and thirdly they must not be markedly old-fashioned. You will see that this limits the choice of words very much indeed . . . 'Back' is not pretty, but it gives that feeling of physical constraint which I want.
>
> (Letter to Robert Bridges, 4 November 1882)

8 **wisdom is early to despair** the wise despair first, since they are the first to see how transient beauty is.

Golden Echo

1 **Spare!** rhyme picked up from the six-fold repetition of *despair* (15–16) at the close of *The Leaden Echo*. Is the exclamation itself used to signal a dramatic change in mood here?

9 **dangerously** the idea of physical beauty as both aesthetically compelling and morally corrupting, a theme to which Hopkins often returns (see comments in the Notes to the late sonnet *To what serves Mortal Beauty?*, pp. 85–6).

26 **fagged** worn out.
   fashed (Scots term) careworn.
   cogged old word for deceived, betrayed.

27 **the thing** physical beauty itself; lines 27–30 involve reference to the Catholic doctrine of the Resurrection, the existence of the redeemed after the Last Judgement will involve a perfection of their physical form as well as their souls.

Ribblesdale

Hopkins suggested this sonnet was a companion to *In the Valley of the Elwy*, p. 17. He also commented in a letter that *it is to be read very pausingly* . . . How do you think the theme or subject matter you find here goes along with this *very pausingly* idea?

One manuscript version of the poem is prefaced by the words of St Paul in the *Epistle to the Romans*, 8, 19–20, a passage concerned with the effects on nature of the morally fallen and corrupt state of mankind. So, nature troubled by the Fall, a poem to be *read very pausingly*, a title referring to a wild part of the Lancashire landscape which Hopkins grew to admire. As so often in Hopkins' sonnets, the sestet develops an explicitly human focus where the octet stays nearer to 'natural' expectations encouraged by the sonnet's title.

 1 **throng**   meant here as an adjective, a Lancashire dialect word again, meaning 'crowded'.
 2 **touched**   dialect, meaning 'slouched', but maybe better suited to the sound patterns of line 2 with *l* sounds stressed in *low* and *appeal*.
 10 **heir**   links with *Genesis* 1, 26–30, humanity *given dominion over the whole earth*; echoing the 'ecological' Hopkins of *Binsey Poplars*?
 11 **selfbent**   absorbed by selfish desires.
 12 **reave**   rob, plunder (as in *Peace*, p. 28 [7]).
 13–14 Human indifference making the earth troubled, pre-occupied (*brows of such care*).

The Blessed Virgin compared to the Air we Breathe

The first things you might notice about this poem, besides its very explicit, explanatory-looking title, are its length and its rhythmical character. At 126 lines it is the third longest poem in this selection, structurally very different from the closely crafted sonnet form to which Hopkins so often returns. And rhythmically, the short line, technically iambic trimeter, giving three feet to the line in a mixture of rhyming couplets and triplets, gives a brisk, clipped effect, again contrasted with the complex rhythms and counter rhythms found elsewhere in this selection.

These departures from Hopkins' norms may be partly explained by the circumstances surrounding the poem's composition. In 1883 Hopkins was teaching at Stonyhurst, the Jesuit seminary in Lancashire. It was a custom at the college for poems in honour of the Virgin Mary to be displayed before her statue during May, her month in the Church calendar. This custom provided the immediate stimulus for the poem.

5   **-flixed**   from 'flix', a kind of animal fur.

24   **Mary Immaculate**   the doctrine that Mary the mother of Christ alone among mankind was born without stain of original sin.

27   **Great as no goddess's**   contrasting true religion from the myths of pre-Christian cultures.

39   **Mantles**   covers and protects, as under a 'mantle', a woman's loose cloak.

42   **almoner**   one responsible for dispensing alms, charity for the poor. Hopkins goes on to say that Mary is less the dispenser of charity from God to man than one form of that divine charity itself.

48   **ghostly**   as often, spiritual.

60   **Nazareths**   linked to *Bethlems* (63, 65); Christ was conceived in Nazareth and born in a stable in Bethlehem.

73–126   Possibly the most rewarding facet of the text for readers whose sympathies may not be greatly stirred by the Catholic doctrine of the Virgin. Between lines 73–113 Hopkins develops an ambitious analogy, both scientific and imaginative. As the sun's impact is mediated by the earth's atmosphere, producing refracted light that allows us to see the rich blue of the sky, so Hopkins suggests here that Mary is the *atmosphere* (115) mediating between imperfect humans and the unbearable majesty of God. Even if you are unmoved by the theology, the image integrates the physical universe, human perception and Hopkins' sense of the presence of God.

80   **Charged**   again the use of a word with electrical, energy-filled associations (look back at its use in the sonnet, *God's Grandeur*, p. 15).

101 **Quartz-fret** a gem cut so as to allow many piercing light points to show.

117 **wend** journey, travel; (see *The Loss of the Eurydice*, p. 24 [101].)

126 The alliterations stress the theme contained in the key epithet *world-mothering air* (1, 124); according to the 'Marian' doctrine in which Hopkins believed, Mary was the mother of all mankind, not of Christ alone, and so the one perfect, morally pure woman to whom all might turn for spiritual comfort.

'To seem the stranger'

Counted amongst the so-called 'Sonnets of Desolation' (see Approaches, pp. 131–3). The theme, announced in line 1, is Hopkins' experience of estrangement: homesick for England, doing a job he finds uncongenial and exhausting, spiritually troubled by the sense that he can no longer communicate with God, the sonnet becomes a medium for exploring the poet's distress and the factors behind it.

2 **Father and mother dear** remember that Hopkins came from a prosperous middle class family, strongly Anglican in their religion. The poet's conversion to Catholicism and decision to become a Catholic priest must have created real dilemmas of understanding and acceptance for them.

4 **he my peace/my parting** *he* is Christ; Hopkins' experience of belief is not one of reassurance but of 'the long night of the soul', distress and insecurity.

8 **wars** the contemporary Irish struggle for political freedom from Britain; Hopkins saw the legitimacy of that struggle, recognizing that he was in an unhappy and turbulent country.

9–10 **third/Remove** isolated by a three-fold exile; from parents, country, and an audience appreciative of his poetic powers.

11–14 The reference is to difficulties over prayer: Hopkins feels unable to pray, doubtful about whether those prayers he does manage ever reach their intended audience. This sharpens the sense of spiritual dejection.

'I wake and feel'

Another of the 'Sonnets of Desolation'. As before, the focus of distress is on the inability to communicate effectively with God, the spiritual pain now aggravated by insomnia and nightmares. Indeed, the sestet ends on a note of real despair; Hopkins likens his torment to that of the damned souls in Hell.

- 1 **fell** blow, but also the idea of an animal pelt, savage and alien.
- 2 **we** Hopkins talking to his *heart* (3) as a fellow-sufferer.
- 7 **like dead letters sent** an evocative simile, because it is so everyday; Hopkins feels like the lover whose letters are sent to the 'dead letter office' because his beloved has moved away and correspondence cannot be forwarded.
- 9–11 **I am gall ... the curse** the image behind the first triplet in this sestet is of the poet as a pain made concrete or material; he doesn't *feel* agony as something that might go away as it came, he *is* agony, a flesh and blood version of the experience itself.
- 12 **Selfyeast** human personality like a bread whose quality depends on the yeast (*spirit*) which causes dull ingredients like flour and water to become nourishing; the stress on 'self' is crucial in a poem full of self-disgust. For further discussion of this poem see Approaches pp. 131–2.

'No worst'

Whereas the sense of distress in the previous two poems involves exploration of the poet's own agitated mental state, here a new element of questioning appears alongside that introspection. If the God in whom Hopkins believes is a God of love, why is the poet allowed to suffer so keenly? The sestet goes on to examine further the mental torment Hopkins is enduring, the imagery evoking vertigo. The symptoms depicted are so extreme that the stark ending hardly comes as a surprise; even so, the suicidal hints retain a strong sense of shock, coming as they do from a priest whose faith placed suicide amongst the most terrible of all sins. For further discussion of the poem see Approaches pp. 131–2.

- 1 **No worst, there is none** notice the abrupt beginning, as if we

are in the middle of an intimate conversation (compare with
Felix Randal, p. 29). What is the effect of saying *worst* here
rather than 'worse'?

pitched   two senses; thrown, but also tuning a stringed
instrument.

2   **forepangs**   previous pains.

3   **Comforter**   the Holy Spirit.

5   **herds-long**   strong metaphor; with *heave* suggesting cries of
pain produced only with great effort, we can imagine here the
moans of cattle in distress, dumb and incapable of finding any
remedy for their suffering.

7–8   **'ling-/Ering!'**   does the stretched out effect of the line-break
perhaps suggest a black kind of word-play?

8   **fell**   the adjective 'deadly', not the noun form as in the opening
line of '*I wake and feel*' (p. 39).

force   contraction of 'perforce', necessarily.

9   **mind, mind**   probably a simple repetition of the noun, al-
though the second *mind* may also have the sense 'look', 'note'.

fall   the vertigo idea; the sound is a deliberate echo in half-
rhyme of *fell* in the preceding line.

12   **Durance**   another contraction, of 'endurance'.

13   **a comfort**   the idea developed in the final line; *death*, or its
temporary version, *sleep*, puts an end to mental suffering, though
remember the sense of insomnia suggested in '*I wake and feel*'.

To what serves Mortal Beauty?

The ideas in this sonnet explore some of Hopkins' most serious
preoccupations. The question giving the sonnet its title and driving
force was bound to be one especially urgent to a mind such as
Hopkins'; with such intense apprehension of the beautiful in nature,
including fellow human beings, coupled to belief in an all-powerful
and judging God, it was inevitable that Hopkins felt the need to
argue out the relationship proper between full awareness of natural
beauty and obedience to God. Remarks in a letter written to Robert
Bridges in 1879, almost six years earlier, offer a useful gloss:

> I think then no one can admire beauty of the body more than I do,
> and it is of course a comfort to find beauty in a friend or a friend in
> beauty. But this kind of beauty is dangerous. Then comes beauty of

the mind, such as genius, and this is greater than beauty of the
body and not to call dangerous. And more beautiful than the beauty
of the mind is beauty of character, the 'handsome heart'.

(Letter to Robert Bridges, 1879)

Physical beauty can be *dangerous* (1) because it offers temptation,
arousing the passions. Such loss of rational control, giving way to
instinctive behaviour, is the spiritual opposite to the life most desired
by the believer, living by grace, resisting temptation to sin. More
than that, Hopkins believed that *mortal beauty* (1) could itself bring
about the death of the soul. Note that the adjective *Mortal* in the
title has more than one sense: not only 'something that will die', but
also 'deadly', 'causing death'.

The thought-process in this closely-reasoned poem approximates
to this: beauty can be dangerous, exciting the passion; but, so long as
its perception is a means to an end, and not a sensual end in itself,
such beauty can be instructive; the example of Pope Gregory (see
Note to line 7); it is right to love the beauty of fellow humans, as the
most complete *mortal beauty* (1) created by God; but the correct way
to cope with such beauty, potentially corrupting, is to see it for what
it is, one kind of evidence for divine power and goodness, of an
inferior kind; by contrast, divine grace itself offers the most complete
beauty of all, the only beauty we might beneficially aim to possess.

2 **O-seal-that-so I feature**   a face so perfect we might want to
preserve it from any subsequent change.

3 **Purcell tune**   see Notes to *Henry Purcell* sonnet, (pp. 75–6).

4–5 **glance ... gaze**   difference between the two important for the
argument developed here.

7 **Gregory**   Pope Gregory (c. A.D.600). The story is that seeing
Britons on sale in a Roman market Gregory exclaimed *Non
Angli, sed Angeli* ('They're angels, not Britons!'). Seeing these
Angli inspired him to send St Augustine (of Canterbury) on a
mission to convert England to Christianity.

8 **that day's dear chance**   the conversion of England apparently
traced back to a lucky accident.

11 **Self flashes off frame and face**   self is most readily perceived in
appearance? So human beauty is closest to divine beauty in
nature? *Self* links directly to the individual's **inscape**. (See
Approaches p. 121).

12 **own**   acknowledge, admit (read with *heaven's sweet gift*, [13]).

14 Would that those you recognize as beautiful might yet achieve that highest condition of beauty, the spiritual beauty given by divine grace? Is this line itself a kind of prayer, apt culmination for a Jesuit's reflections on beauty, sin and salvation?

(Carrion Comfort)

Here as elsewhere, the title is bracketed simply because Hopkins left the poem without a title; the brackets indicate the title is the work of his first editor, Robert Bridges.

The starting point of the sonnet is a dialogue with *Despair* (1), one of the seven deadly sins, which Hopkins sees as offering him an easy but fatal release from his spiritual turmoil. Again perhaps there are the suicidal implications suggested at the end of 'No worst'. The difference is that this poem begins, with its fourfold repetition of the defiant *Not*, in a more vigorous mood of rejection. Despair is the terminal state of hopelessness, what remains when belief has disappeared. Hopkins insists that belief remains, however difficult it has become since God has chosen to test the poet by withdrawing from him. For us as readers the relationship between octet and sestet presents the real challenges of interpretation here. For further discussion of this poem see Approaches pp. 132–3.

1 **carrion comfort**   *carrion* is decaying/loathsome flesh; *comfort* consolation or food. The phrase, describing *Despair*, can be read as both 'comfort to carrion' and 'deriving comfort from carrion'.

4 **not choose not to be**   deny the attraction of death and oblivion. *Not* is employed six times in four lines; is Hopkins maybe protesting too much here, as if what he strenuously denies might just have more of a grip on him than he dares admit?

5 **rude**   adverb; rudely, brutally.

6 **wring-earth**   characteristic invention, a strong compound adjective suggesting the world shaking force of the power that assaults Hopkins.

 rock   verb, going with *wouldst* (5).

9 **Why?**   key word; why is despair so concerned to claim the poet's soul? The octet has graphically described the attacks of

despair, and the questions have a real theological edge; why is God allowing the poet to be so tempted? In the sestet Hopkins attempts a coherent answer, a way of justifying God's refusal to intervene. You need to decide for yourself how effective that answer is, and how well it works with the ideas of the octet.

10   **coil**   tumult, uproar.

kissed the rod   biblical image of submission to divine punishment and correction; despite his submission, Hopkins has felt no relief from torment. The image of the divine *rod* also figures in the sonnet *God's Grandeur*, (p. 15 [4]) as well as in *The Wreck of the Deutschland*, (p. 3 [10]).

12   **hero**   Christ?

14   **(my God!)**   the believer's shock at realizing that his struggle is with God himself; the wrestling, struggling motif has strong echoes of the Old Testament, in particular *Genesis* 32, where Jacob wrestles with the angel.

'Patience, hard thing'

Look again at the earlier curtal sonnet, *Peace*, (p. 28) where Hopkins develops the idea of *Patience exquisite* (8) as the precursor, the forerunner, of Peace itself. In the context of these 'Sonnets of Desolation' the decision to focus here on patience – endurance, readiness to wait and suffer (the Latin verb *patior* contains both senses) – is significant. In one of his devotional writings, the *Comments on the Spiritual Exercises of St Ignatius Loyola*, Hopkins advises: *Let him who is in desolation strive to remain in patience, which is the virtue contrary to the troubles which harass him; and let him think that he will shortly be consoled, making diligent efforts against the desolation.* The octet develops the idea that patience is itself the result of suffering or misfortune, whilst the sestet suggests that for human *hearts* (9) to accommodate themselves to God's will demands a readiness to suffer pain. Whether the thoughts explored in the sonnet are convincing, whether they articulate an experience Hopkins had now at last actually felt, or was something he still desperately longed for, this is for you to decide yourself. Certainly the tone offers a marked contrast to the blackness evoked by several of the previous sonnets.

1–4 Someone who asks for patience is also implicitly taking on the spiritual pain and discomfort it entails.

6 **No-where** *Rare patience* (5) is associated exclusively with want, misfortune, suffering.

ivy the metaphor is visually striking; capacity to endure masks the ruined structure of our previous existence.

8 **Purple eyes** berries.

10 **dearer** an anachronism, used in the sense 'more seriously' as well as in the commoner sense 'more valuable'.

12 **distills** drops, lets fall (especially of honey).

13 **He** Christ.

14 **combs** honeycombs.

'My own heart'

Here the mood differs from that found in previous poems in the 'Sonnets of Desolation' sequence. There is less of an accent on describing distress, more interest in how to establish the conditions which might help the poet regain equanimity and calm. Where does he hope to rediscover such peace? It is left unspoken, but the final image of the sonnet provides a haunting glimpse of natural beauty, a sense of the **inscape** in creation (see Approaches pp. 118–20), pointedly absent from the other poems in this sequence.

3–4 Does the tortured syntax here heighten or mock the sense of torment?

5–8 This second quatrain is compressed so the meanings can be hard to get at. You probably need to insert a word like 'world' after *comfortless* (6) and read the *world of wet* (8) as a Hopkins coinage – characteristically highlighted through alliteration – for the sea, undrinkable water.

9 **poor Jackself** other texts use *Jack* as a dismissive term for plain, everyday human nature. (See *That Nature is a Heraclitean Fire and of the comfort of the Resurrection* p. 47 [23] and *The Shepherd's Brow* p. 48 [11].)

11 **root-room** the metaphor, significantly, taken from nature and organic growth; *comfort* seen as a plant that might yet *root* in the soul.

11 **size**   grow.

14 **Betweenpie**   a striking coinage; Hopkins is using a verb, 'to pie', in the sense to possess variegated colouring (see *Pied Beauty* p. 19). Adding 'between' to create the compound term probably gives the word the sense 'making things appear alternately light and dark'. Skies often have this effect on mountains when the sun's rays are intermittently blocked by cloud. We are made to work for the meaning Hopkins is creating here.

Spelt from Sibyl's Leaves

Like the night scene which, in part, it aims to describe, this sonnet can appear dark and dense. It evokes sunset and the beginnings of night; out of this develop thoughts about the implications for human consciousness. As elsewhere, the octet, sestet relationship can be seen in terms of physical evocation leading the poet's mind to spiritual, ethical reflection. The characteristic development is from inanimate nature to human existence and its links with the divine, creative powers sustaining the world.

The actual title is (intentionally?) puzzling and oblique. *Spelt*, in connection with the Sibyl and her Leaves, suggests divination: the interpretation of omens in order to foretell future events. In ancient mythology the Sibylline Leaves were the palm leaves on which prophecies about the end of the world were written in Greek. In the medieval Latin hymn about the Last Judgement, the *Dies Irae* (Day of Wrath), the Sibyl is mentioned as an authority who has foreseen the terrors of that day. Time will end and God will sit in judgement on all human beings, judging some to join him in paradise for eternity, others to experience the everlasting torments of hell. The sestet is heavily coloured by such powerful ideas of judgement and damnation.

Hopkins recognized the dramatic qualities of this sonnet and its subject matter. Throughout, the lines are extended, giving an impression of a much longer poem, even though it is without the codas he used to lengthen other late sonnets (see Notes to *Harry Ploughman* p.92). Hopkins was sensitive to the need for effective recitation too as seen in this comment to Bridges:

above all remember what applies to all my verse, that it is, as living
art should be, made for performance and that its performance is not
reading with the eye but loud, leisurely, poetical (not rhetorical)
recitation, with long rests, long dwells on the rhyme and other
marked syllables ... This sonnet shd. be almost sung ...

(Letter to Robert Bridges, 11 December 1886)

1 A sense of drama from the start: the opening line is a sequence
   of multi-syllabled adjectives, and nothing else, employed to
   qualify *Evening* at the start of the second line, a tantalizing
   build-up.

   Earnest   high, lofty.

   attuneable   able to be harmonized, a Hopkins coinage.

   stupendous   literally, causing terror and amazement.

3 **hornlight ... hoarlight**   yellow glow from a lantern; greyish-
   white glow as from hoarfrost.

4 **Waste**   fade.

   earlstars   major stars of the visible constellations.

5 **dapple**   the mix and mingling of things – lights, textures,
   colours; (see *dappled things* [1] *Pied Beauty* p. 19).

6 **throughther**   contraction for 'throughout her', i.e. the earth?

   self   individual self-consciousness, as elsewhere, a central
   issue.

7 **Disremembering**   forgetting, another dialect term.

9 **dragonish**   dragons symbolize the dark forces evoked in the
   Book of Revelation as the final conflict between good and evil
   occurs at the end of time.

   damask   a verb, literally to put ornate (arabic) patterns on a
   sword-blade.

10 **our oracle!**   In Virgil's Latin epic poem *The Aeneid* the hero,
   Aeneas, is led into the underworld by the Sibyl of Cumae to see
   his dead father.

11 **part, pen, pack**   the basic idea is the sorting of the sheep from
   the goats (see *St Matthew's Gospel*, 25), the elect going to
   Heaven, the damned going to Hell at the Last Judgement (so
   flocks ... folds, [12]).

13 **ware**   aware of or beware!

14 **selfwrung, selfstrung**   dramatic images of Hell as Hopkins
   conceived it. His own depressions led him to reflect with
   personal engagement on the idea that the ultimate torture was

the fact of permanent estrangement from God's love. Hell, the place of punishment, becomes the eternally isolated and lonely *self*, tortured by its own unending thoughts of loss and regret (see 'My own heart', p. 42 [3–4] for a similar perception, there applied explicitly to Hopkins' own situation).

Harry Ploughman

Like *Tom's Garland*, the next poem in this selection, and the sonnet *That Nature is a Heraclitean Fire and of the comfort of the Resurrection*, Hopkins expands the sonnet form considerably here by a series of codas. The result: a sonnet some way over 14 lines long, which still retains the statement development relationship between its elements which characterizes most of Hopkins' sonnets. As with more conventional sonnets, only four rhymes are used throughout. This use of codas marks the opposite process from the condensing approach employed earlier in the 'curtal' sonnets *Pied Beauty* and *Peace*.

In a letter, Hopkins said that he had written *a direct picture of a ploughman, without afterthought*. After stressing that it was composed *for recital and not for perusal* (see his comments on performance, in the Notes to *Spelt from Sibyl's Leaves*, pp. 90–1), he commented that *perhaps it will strike you as intolerably violent and artificial*. Does this suggestion of violence, artificiality, echo any of your own reactions to this sonnet? Have you found any more to the poem than highly involved description?

1 **hurdle**   willow twigs twisted into portable fencing.
  broth   a strange word here?
  Flue   is an old term for down, so here, probably, 'hair'.
2 **rack of ribs**   ribcage.
3 **Rope-over thigh**   visual image of rope-like thigh muscles?
  knee-nave   kneecap (an old sense of 'nave' is the hub of a wheel).
7 **onewhere**   in one place; in another place.
  curded   becoming knotted, bunched, muscles vividly compared to milk becoming like curd.
9 **beechbole**   trunk of a beech tree, often used for ships' masts because of their combination of strength and straightness,

qualities here applied to the ploughman.

rollcall like *crew* (5) this suggests the various limbs and muscle groups as the component members of a military unit, working effectively only when under the command of a single leader. St Paul's image of believers as the constituent parts of the body of Christ (*Epistle to the Romans*, 12, 4–5) may also be relevant here.

14 **crossbridle** tangle (of the plough's reins).

15 **lilylocks** blond hair.

16 **Churlsgrace** the natural grace of the peasant; it might be helpful to look again at Hopkins' reflections on physical grace in the sonnet, *To what serves Mortal Beauty?* (p. 40).

it i.e. the *churlsgrace*; controlling his feet as they race over the earth behind the plough (*cragiron*, [18]).

Amansstrength what might be Hopkins' reasons for contracting three words into one here?

Tom's Garland

Here Hopkins sustains a level of complexity in both thought and technique that led his early admirers to expressions of bafflement. As with the previous poem, codas are used to extend the physical range of the sonnet, now twenty lines, while the verbal technique becomes progressively more cryptic and condensed. Whether the style points to the direction Hopkins' poetry would have taken had he lived longer it is impossible to say; it may be significant that in his very last poem, *To R.B.* (p. 48) he reverts to a more accessible, even traditional approach to the sonnet.

The puzzlement of his contemporaries has had one helpful outcome for later readers, however, in that it provoked Hopkins into 'unpacking' the ideas within the sonnet in his correspondence. Before setting out his own paraphrase of the sonnet, Hopkins expressed regret about the lack of comprehension in his two readers, Robert Bridges and the Anglican priest R. W. Dixon:

> It is plain I must go no further on this road: if you and he cannot understand me, who will? Yet, declaimed, the strange constructions would be dramatic and effective.
>
> (Letter to Robert Bridges, 10 February 1888)

Notice the stress here on *declaimed*, like the comments Hopkins made about performance in connection with *Spelt from Sibyl's Leaves* and *Harry Ploughman* (see Notes pp. 90–1 and p. 92), it clearly underlines the importance he attached to the aural dimension in poetry, its 'musicality', the sensuous dimension of verse spoken aloud and heard (see also Approaches p. 112).

It is probably best to regard what Hopkins goes on to say in this letter as 'scaffolding' to help with your own reading of this poem. His comments certainly do not – and were never meant to – exhaust all the possible meanings which readers can discover in the poem. They simply offer an orientation as to Hopkins' preoccupations:

> ... the commonwealth or well-ordered human society is like one man; a body with many members and each its function; some higher, some lower, but all honourable, from the honour which belongs to the whole. The head is the sovereign ... we must then imagine this head as bare ... and covered ... only with the sun and stars, of which the crown is a symbol; it has an enormous hat or skull cap, the vault of heaven. The foot is the daylabourer ... armed with hobnail boots, because it has to wear and be worn by the ground; which again is symbolical; for it is navvies or daylabourers who ... mainly trench, tunnel, blast, and in other ways disfigure, 'mammock' the earth and ... stamp it with their footprints ...
> Therefore the scene of the poem is laid at evening, when they are giving over work and one after another pile their picks ... knocking sparks out of mother earth not now by labour ... but by the mere footing ... Here ... the action of the mind mimics that of the labourer – surveys his lot, low but free from care; then by a sudden strong act throws it over the shoulder ...
>
> (Letter to Robert Bridges, 10 February 1888)

1 **garlanded**   *And the garlands of nails they wear are therefore the visible badge of the place they fill, the lowest in the commonweath ...* i.e. the studded sole of Tom's workboot.
2 **fallowbootfellow**   a contraction/invention for a workmate (*bootfellow*) whose labour is for the time being over (*fallow*).
3 **rockfire**   sparks.
9 **lacklevel**   absence of equality, equal shares in goods or wealth.
12 **no way sped**   no way assisted, helped.
15 **Undenizened**   outcast, homeless.

19–20 The thought in this final couplet has an explicit social and political message behind it, best expressed by Hopkins in his letter:

> But presently I remember that this is all very well for those who are in, however low in, the Commonwealth and share in any way in the common weal; but that the curse of our times is that many do not share it, that they are outcasts from it and have neither security nor splendour; that they share care with the high and obscurity with the low, but wealth or comfort with neither. And this state of things, I say, is the origin of Loafers, Tramps, Cornerboys, Roughs, Socialists and other pests of society.
>
> (Letter to Robert Bridges, 10 February 1888)

Those alienated from society through unemployment either despair and grow apathetic (*Hangdog dull*) or, worse, become angrily disaffected, revolutionaries and malcontents (*Manwolf*). Hopkins has no remedies, but from direct personal experience – not least from his time in a poor Liverpool parish – he recognizes the malignant repercussions of unemployment. Much earlier than this, in August 1871, he commented in a letter to Robert Bridges that he felt the aims, if not the means, of communism were just:

> ... it is a dreadful thing for the greatest and most necessary part of a very rich nation to live a hard life without dignity, knowledge, comforts, delight, or hopes in the midst of plenty – which plenty they make. They profess that they do not care what they wreck and burn, the old civilization and order must be destroyed. This is a dreadful look out but what has the old civilization done for them?

That Nature is a Heraclitean Fire and of the comfort of the Resurrection

An arresting title for an arresting poem. Alongside *Tom's Garland* and *Harry Ploughman*, this poem represents the most ambitious of Hopkins' experiments with the sonnet as a poetic form. Like those other poems, it confronts its readers with a variety of challenges and potential pleasures: technique pushed further than ever, dizzy exuberance in the language and imagery, and densely original lines of thought.

Two basic pulses emerge: Hopkins' sense of the transience and diversity of natural phenomena, dazzlingly captured in the opening nine lines; and his conviction that in a universe prolific with such finite, unstable phenomena, belief in Christ's resurrection alone offers the soul of man the chance of an eternal, stable existence. You might interpret all of this as the anguish and doubt of the 'Sonnets of Desolation' seemingly transcended and conquered by the bubbling energy of a sonnet confidently linking an early Greek scientific thinker and the essential Christian doctrine of redemption. But it might just be a desperate attempt to regain equilibrium, after the suicidal depths of those poems, through verbal and intellectual gymnastics. Which seems the more plausible reading?

1 **chevy** scamper, chase.
3 **roughcast** lime and gravel for coating walls, often painted over with whitewash.
4 **Shivelights** splinters of light.
shadowtackle another invention; patterns of shadow?
6–7 A precisely organized description of the process by which mud eventually reverts to dust.
8 **Squadroned** from armies of boots?
9 **Footfretted** invention again; patterns in earth made by passing feet.
Million-fueled Heraclitus' ideas are known only through a few surviving fragments; in one of them he refers to the earth as a huge bonfire (fragment 220).
10 **clearest-selved** *self* and *selve* are important terms for Hopkins; mankind is here seen as the most individualized, personally distinctive, item in the created universe (look again at the sonnet *As kingfishers catch fire*, p. 16 especially line 7).
13–14 **that shone/Sheer off, disseveral** again, each human personality a brilliant star, each quite distinct (*disseveral*).
15 **stark** strong, firm.
18 You have only to think back to the contexts of Hopkins' two most ambitious poems to appreciate his horror of shipwreck and drowning. Here the metaphor is of a man's life as a ship in danger, the promise held out by Christ's resurrection a

lighthouse signal, *A beacon, an eternal beam*, (19) the one chance of eventual safety.

20 **residuary**   remaining; overtones of death and decay increased by the word's associations with wills or legacies.

22 The central Christian doctrine which erupts so often into Hopkins' poetry; the incarnation, God becoming a human in the person of Christ, as the central fact of all history, the fact that makes possible an eternal existence with God for the human soul.

23 **This Jack, joke, poor potsherd, patch**   the chiming effect of 'Cynghannedd' is conspicuous here (see Approaches p. 110). As elsewhere *Jack* (see Notes to line 9 of '*My own heart*', p. 89) used as a shorthand for the typical, fallen human being, a kind of 'everyman'; *potsherd* is a broken piece or shard of earthenware, used in the *Book of Job* as an image of humanity as a flawed aspect of creation. The sharpness is enhanced by alliteration and the chiming effect of *Jack, joke* (Hopkins is dismissive of himself here) whilst *patch* is an old term for a fool, a twit.

23–4 **immortal diamond**   the contrast is dramatic; from *mortal trash* (19), *joke . . . patch . . . matchwood* (23) to the idea of something precious, brilliant, enduring for eternity. One of Hopkins' most powerful conclusions, or an over-dramatized ending, too reliant on violent extremes in the imagery?

Justus quidem tu es, Domine,

The Latin epigraph that forms the title partially translated in line 1, is from the Old Testament prophet, *Jeremiah* 12, 1, where God is taken to task for his apparent lack of justice or fair play. *You are indeed just lord if I argue with you; yet argue I must; why do the affairs of the wicked prosper . . . ?* The directness with which Hopkins addresses God here, variously imploring, reproaching and querying, results in a text of uncharacteristic explicitness. You might even want to think about it in dramatic terms, as a monologue.

Writing to Robert Bridges in March 1889 soon after completing the poem, Hopkins commented that *it must be read* adagio molto [very slowly] *and with great stress.* Bridges was later to speak of the sonnet as *an address to God, most powerful and plaintive.* Only in *The Wreck of the Deutschland* does Hopkins set out as here by directly addressing God; there is a much less provocative, dramatic invocation at the start of *The Loss of the Eurydice* (see Notes to both poems pp. 50–62 and pp. 70–73). The vocabulary employed to address God is also significant: *Lord* (1), *sir* (2), *thou my friend* (5), *thou lord of life* (14). What part do these very different terms play in the moods of the sonnet? And what might the whole poem suggest about Hopkins' state of mind during the spring of his last year?

The questioning of divine justice we read in the *Book of Jeremiah* and again at the start of the sonnet is called 'theodicy'. On what grounds does Hopkins seem to be questioning that justice here?

4 **Disappointment** the key 'tonal' word of the poem? See comments on line 13.

7 **sots and thralls** (drunken) fools and slaves.

9 **brakes** thickets.

11 **fretty chervil** cow parsley with serrated leaves.

13 **Time's eunuch** *Gospel of St Matthew* 19, 12 speaks of those who *become as eunuchs for the kingdom of God*. Hopkins uses the term meaning an emasculated, so sterile, servant, to evoke his sense of his condition. To be *Time's eunuch* involves the idea of being an unproductive slave of mortality itself, conscious of life passing with goals unrealized. The phrase conveys a sense of futility, even maybe of self-contempt. Writing to Bridges in January 1888, Hopkins refers to himself as a *eunuch – but it is for the kingdom of heaven's sake*. In the same letter he declares *all impulse fails me: I can give myself no sufficient reason for going on. Nothing comes* ... An earlier letter to Bridges, from September 1885, includes the graphic and candid revelation *... it kills me to be time's eunuch and never to beget*. Most powerfully of all, just three months prior to writing this sonnet, Hopkins disclosed in notes written on New Year's Day 1889 a desolating sense of personal failure:

What is my wretched life? Five wasted years have passed almost in Ireland. I am ashamed of the little I have done ... All my undertakings miscarry: I am like a straining eunuch. I wish then for death: yet if I died now I should die imperfect, no master of myself, and that is the worst failure of all. O my God, look down on me.

from Sermons and Devotional Writings

'The shepherd's brow'

Written in the final months of his life, like the sonnets *Justus quidem tu es, Domine* and *To R.B.*, Hopkins seems preoccupied here with expressing a mood of disaffection with mankind: at fallen, corrupt human nature, and especially at himself as one embodiment of it. The mood is bleak and unforgiving; the joyful vision of creation which animates so many of the previous poems in this selection has, temporarily or otherwise, been replaced by a dark and cynical view of the world. The disparaging, self-deprecatory tone is particularly well caught in the final couplet.

Robert Bridges, Hopkins' first editor, did not take to this poem at all. He set it aside in his edition of 1918 with the unfinished poems and fragments, arguing that ... *this must have been thrown off one day in a cynical mood, which he would not have wished to intrude among his last serious poems.* This might form a good starting point for discussion: how far as a reader would you want to argue for or against Bridges' judgement?

1 **fronting** confronting, facing up to.
   owns not possesses, more likely acknowledges, admits (like own up).
3 **Angels** the fall of the rebellious angels from Heaven.
5 **scaffold** in the senses of 'framework' and 'place of execution'; look again at the opening of *The Caged Skylark*, (p. 19).
7 *memento mori* literally, a reminder of one's death.
8 **bass** lowest part in a harmony, but also 'base' as in vile, low?
   viol medieval stringed instrument, precursor of violin, cello etc. In some translations of the Old Testament, the word is used to describe a harp or lyre which accompanied mourning or lamentation.
11 **Jack** look again at the use of this term in the sonnets 'My own heart' (p. 42) and *That Nature is a Heraclitean Fire and of the comfort of the Resurrection* (p. 46) in each instance, a kind of shorthand for sinful human nature.
   mate implying relationships between men and women reduced to their most basic, reproductive terms?
   hussy derived from 'housewife', and presumably meant by Hopkins as a female counterpart to *Jack*.

13 **masque** dramatic and musical entertainment; with the implication that human existence is a meaningless show, a worthless fiction.

To R. B.

This is Hopkins' last poem, written in April 1889, just seven weeks before his final illness and death. Again, note the return to a traditional sonnet formula in terms of its length, and the syntax and rhythms employed. R. B. is Robert Bridges, whom Hopkins first met as an undergraduate at Oxford (they were both born in 1844) and with whom Hopkins corresponded from 1865 until his death. The mood here contrasts tellingly with that of the previous poem, despite the fact that both were written about the same time – something which may well have influenced Bridges in his attitude to the status of that poem in his 1918 edition, (see p. 99).

This is a special poem in Hopkins' output, and not just because it is his last. It is the one surviving poem in which he celebrates his own creativity, however fitful, as a writer, the ecstasy of inspiration and its painful infrequency. Whereas the sonnet *Justus quidem tu es, Domine*, from the same year laments spiritual and creative drought, here the tone adopted is gentler, more resigned. After the dramatic spiritual and emotional landscapes drawn in many of his other later sonnets, Hopkins offers his friend and supporter a sense of his own hard-won equanimity, his acceptance of creative genius as a two-edged gift from God. It would be futile to speculate about the extent to which Hopkins knew he had little time left to live, but it is hard to read this sonnet without experiencing a strong sense of valediction, of leave-taking. Bridges was himself later to comment in a letter that even if the tone of the sonnet did not explicitly suggest *foreboding*, it was still *full of a strange fitness for the end*.

1–4 The metaphor developed is of the poem as the child of a momentary union between inspiration and the writer's mind; once the seed from the former has fertilized the egg from the latter, a long period of gestation occurs before the actual 'birth'.

6 **combs** grooms, prepares; commentators have discussed at length just how a mother can *comb* her as yet unborn child.

Bridges suggested the revision 'moulds'. Which seems better to you?

7 **widow**   continuing the opening metaphor, the mind now seen as the widow of the momentary inspiration, *The fine delight that fathers thought* of line 1.

9 **muse**   poetry.

10 **want**   both 'desire' and 'lack'.

12 **the roll, the rise, the carol**   terms from ornithology, describing display and mating rituals in the spring. Note the swelling rhythmical effect of lengthening syllables in the line.

13 **My winter world**   Hopkins' own inert and sterile condition as a writer.

Approaches

This part of the book aims to provide you with some guidance as you reflect on Hopkins' poetry and try to make sense of it for yourself. The Approaches start off by focusing on a single text then go on to discuss Hopkins' technique as a poet and the central ideas and themes his poems develop.

Approaches through a study of *The Windhover*

This opening Approach assumes you have read *The Windhover* (p. 18). You might find it helpful to have the poem in front of you as you look at this section.

That meaning relies on context is illustrated by the opening. Because the title refers to a bird of prey, the words *I caught this morning* (1) imply snaring – an ironic association given the subject of the description, a hunting bird. Only from the end of the second line on do we find that the event described is the distinctive flight behaviour of the kestrel. The poet has *caught* (1) the bird only in the sense of glimpsing it unexpectedly for an instant.

Activity

Look at the opening two lines of the poem. How does Hopkins try to grab your attention on reading this text?

Discussion

Some possible starting points might well include:

1 Drama: the poem is immediately personal; it is about someone, the *I* (1) who starts things off. You read of a recent personal experience. Maybe simple curiosity urges you on?
2 Rhythm: fast, urgent? Try reading these lines at a slow pace; it is very difficult! The impetus is headlong; motion is irresistible.
3 Rhyming: the *-ing* sound is conspicuous. Assume it is deliberate;

even if you cannot find a reason for the repetition, at the very least the technique sharpens your attention in reading.

4 Vocabulary: simple and sophisticated. If *minion* (1) and *dauphin* (2) are unfamiliar, look them up then think about a possible link with the word *kingdom* (1–2) which straddles these lines.

5 Sound: look again at the phrase *dapple-dawn-drawn Falcon* (2), alliteration with internal rhythm. The effect is both emphatic and deliberate.

The lines describing the motions of the kestrel suggest a mood verging on intoxication, an observer transfixed by the beauty of the bird's easy movement, keen to capture both that movement and the intense feelings it stirs through the language and rhythms used. The pride identified in the kestrel leads Hopkins to portray him on horseback, a commanding figure ushering in the brilliance of sunlight (*riding . . . striding . . . rung upon the rein* [2–4]). But more than this, the bird's facility indirectly suggests the way the poet regards himself: *My heart in hiding/Stirred for a bird, – the achieve of, the mastery of the thing!* (7–8). An envious longing in the poet-observer? What if the kestrel's flight represents to the poet everything he is not? In that case, this celebration of 'completeness' might be a more complex matter. Something more has happened to the poet than sighting a kestrel's flight: something urgent, especially memorable.

Activity

List some of the reasons why Hopkins seems so attracted to the kestrel. Then think about whether the dedication *to Christ our Lord* makes any difference to the way you read the poem.

Discussion

Reasons for this attraction might include some or all of the following:

1 Aerial virtuosity; ease and authority of motion.
2 Show of power and facility in an environment where the poet has none.
3 Link with start of day; new beginnings and new life, perhaps tied in with bird's energy and grace.
4 Sheer physical beauty of the creature.

What does the dedication add to all of this? It establishes a religious context. We know that the poet is a Christian, with beliefs about the divine informing physical nature yet distinct from it. The final six lines offer the acid test; if you disregard the dedication and anything you may know of the author's life, what interpretation makes most sense of these lines to you: one incorporating some reference to a Christian scheme of values or one which takes the words and images purely at face value?

Transfixed by the beautiful in nature, embodied in the kestrel, the poet-observer is even more stirred by awareness of the supernatural force through which the kestrel's powerful beauty is sustained. A useful term might be Epiphany: a revelation of the divine amidst the everyday realities of transient nature. So if the opening section evokes the 'natural' context, and the first half of this final part suggests elements of 'supernatural' experience within that context, as in an epiphany, what about the final lines?

Is something like an epiphany suggested in lines 13–14? Is the metaphor of lifeless embers from a fire (note the fusion of sound and sense in the alliteration of *blue-bleak* [13]), splitting apart to disclose heat within, a symbol for what an epiphany might be like? Hopkins' meaning remains complex. Colourless, 'dead' embers can break to show heat; but *Fall, gall themselves, and gash gold-vermilion* (14)? Dramatic terms for describing so ordinary a phenomenon as this?

Unless, out of the ordinary can break the extraordinary, from the natural a glimpse of the supernatural. *Vermilion* (14) – blood? Remember the dedication: within the beliefs so important to Hopkins was the claim that Christ, the son of God, sacrificed himself to repair the relationship between mankind and God, nature and supernature. What of the *sheer plod* (12)? As a priest, Hopkins' life was grounded in obedience, submission to authority; perhaps the metaphor of the humdrum plough, given a special sheen through the action of breaking the soil, mirrors his sense of his own outwardly humdrum, routine-driven life?

What have we discovered? A deep awareness of nature, enhanced by a poet aware of his own limits and the unlimited power of God: it seems reasonable to argue that the epiphany from which the lyric sp ings reminds the poet not just of the divine creativity sustaining nature; he is also reminded of his own limitations. Envy at the kestrel's prowess is contained within the believer's sense of the divine; faith insists that his relationship *to Christ our Lord* will save him from the inadequacies he recognizes in himself, inadequacies which the kestrel's flight might only have intensified.

So, one aspect of Hopkins which you might want to test out in the Approaches is that of a writer whose obsession with God in nature acquires special force through boldness of rhythm, of imagery, of sound. That boldness makes his voice utterly distinctive. The aim of the following sections is to help you respond to such qualities in specific contexts, making connections between the distinctive voice and the vision Hopkins articulates through it.

The focus from now on is a special trinity: God, nature and their combined impact on the imagination of the poet, Gerard Manley Hopkins.

Approaches through Hopkins' Poetic Technique

Reading Hopkins

The aim of pages 102–5 was to get you looking in some detail at the techniques Hopkins uses in *The Windhover*, and alongside technique to suggest some of the ideas that stimulated him to write. The assumption was that *The Windhover* could in some senses be seen as a characteristic Hopkins poem, a poem whose technique, structure, tone and themes could also be seen working more widely in his output as a writer.

That opening discussion has highlighted three focal points:

1 the style of the poem, its verbal and rhythmic energy;
2 its stress on nature and religion;
3 the sense a reader can indirectly form of the *I* speaking in the poem.

First, then, a look at style.

Hopkins' Style

The word 'style' when applied to a poet can mean many things. Here it is taken to mean the distinctive way in which Hopkins employs the resources of language, in particular, sound and rhythm, to convey meaning. Because Hopkins was a great experimenter in matters of rhythm and language, it is easy for readers new to him to be intimidated by discussions of technique; learned journals are full of articles on Hopkins' 'prosody', the technical term for the study of rhythm and metre, which can have the effect of making the whole topic seem academic and difficult. In its essentials, it is not; nor is it worth getting too concerned about the finer points of the innovative technique which Hopkins christened **sprung rhythm**. Like all discussion of the 'how' in a poem, thinking about Hopkins' approach to rhythm is justified only where it can be interestingly applied to the 'what', the focus, the theme, the concern. This approach to style will be adopted throughout this section of the Approaches.

Sprung Rhythm

So, **sprung rhythm.** What is it? Why does Hopkins use it?

Activity

Look at the first two stanzas (lines 1–8) of *The Habit of Perfection* (p. 2); read it aloud. Note down any thoughts you have about the rhythm you find there. Then look at the octet (lines 1–8) of the sonnet *Hurrahing in Harvest* (p. 20). Do the same as for the first poem. Are there any differences? Compare your findings if possible with those of other readers.

Discussion

Reading *The Habit of Perfection* I detect a steady four beat rhythm, the kind of metre associated with octosyllabic verse: poems in which each line contains exactly eight syllables. The effect seems light and undemanding, assisted by the regular abab rhyme in each stanza. This choice of rhythm and form necessarily involves compromise over the choice and placing of words; e.g. the phrase *Which only* (8), instead of 'which alone', seems imposed by the rhythmical scheme. The effect is smooth, calm, regular. By contrast, the rhythmical scheme in *Hurrahing in Harvest* seems more disjointed, with syllables in each line varying between ten and fourteen. The lines are therefore longer; punctuation is used to interrupt poetic flow (e.g. semicolons, lines 1–2; exclamations lines 2–3); commas are used liberally, to slow down the tempo, to stress or accent (e.g. lines 5,7). In place of a rhythm which achieves regular flow to suggest something fulfilled or satisfied, this seems like a rhythm imitating someone talking excitedly, pointing out things of importance, suggesting real involvement.

We can say that **sprung rhythm** involves writing lines of poetry in which the number of syllables used matters much less than the organization of stresses: the syllables deliberately chosen for emphasis by the voice. Regularity in regard to the syllabic length of each line, its quantity, becomes secondary; what matters is the regular sequence of stressed syllables, irrespective of the actual count of syllables per line.

There is more to the practice of **sprung rhythm** than this outline indicates; if you are interested in learning more about prosody in Hopkins, the best place to start is the Preface Hopkins wrote to the poems his friend Robert Bridges kept for him in manuscript (unprinted) form. That Preface is reprinted at the head of *The Wreck of the Deutschland* in each of the three complete editions of the poetry listed in the Further Reading section at the end of this book (p. 141). And several of the books of criticism mentioned in that section contain fuller treatments of this aspect of Hopkins' technique. The questions which arise here are: why did he employ this technique, and what does it do for his poems?

Two earlier poems in this selection, *Heaven-Haven* and *The Habit of Perfection*, include no traces of this stress-based rhythmical understanding; the majority of the poems written from the mid 1870s onwards, starting with *The Wreck of the Deutschland*, use this technique in increasingly ambitious ways. In returning to a rhythmic pattern which he alleged linked together classical and medieval poetry, nursery rhymes and the natural rhythm of human speech, Hopkins seems to have regarded himself as a mixture of innovator and traditionalist. In doing something with rhythm not generally exploited in English verse since Elizabethan times, he establishes his claim to stylistic originality by rediscovering a technique which links together common speech rhythm and centuries of verse rhythm.

Why does he do it? Speculation can be entertaining, but at this point it is perhaps premature. No one can say what prompted Hopkins to integrate technical conclusions he drew from reflecting on the way rhythm operated in a range of poets, into the fabric of his own achievement as a poet. In a letter to R.W. Dixon (admirer and former schoolmaster) of October 1878 he commented that *I had long had haunting my ear the echo of a new rhythm which now I realized on paper*. The form that realization of a *haunting . . . new rhythm* took was *The Wreck of the Deutschland*. But *haunting my ear* may be a significant clue; it hardly suggests a deliberate attempt at novelty, writing in a different way just to be different. It sounds more like the unforced, unconscious originality of a creative genius, a radically new way of organizing movement in a poem which comes unbidden to the writer but which he feels compelled to accept and exploit. What do you think?

In terms of 'why?', you will for the moment have to settle for the suggestion made in the Discussion section on pages 106–7; that **sprung rhythm** was a liberating device for a poet working at a time when rules and conventions meant far more than they do in the more *laissez - faire* artistic culture of the late Twentieth century. It allowed Hopkins to introduce a dramatic 'declamatory' quality into his verse, replicating the patterns of natural human speech in a heightened or stylized manner. Discussion later in these Approaches (p. 112) shows how basic to the impact and purpose of his poems Hopkins felt the declamatory element to be: the effect of reading a poem, hearing a poem read aloud. At the same time, Hopkins retained the controlling factor of rhyme. He also held on to traditional structural devices; the majority of texts in this selection are either sonnets or longer poems organized in a formal stanza arrangement. So innovation made within well-observed boundaries; inventive radicalism over rhythm is balanced by employment of accepted poetic forms.

The Sound World

It is not only in his rhythmic adventurousness that we can look at Hopkins as an original, and so think about his style as distinctive. In the sound-world created in his verse, Hopkins reveals an awareness which, like his interest in rhythm, is as much musical as literary. Discussion of *The Windhover* (pp. 102–5) has suggested some of this quality; the aim here is to identify pervasive techniques and offer some ideas about why his verse might incorporate them.

Hopkins uses the techniques of alliteration and assonance, deliberately repeated consonant and vowel sounds respectively, for a variety of reasons. Sometimes it is to suggest a connection between the sound *in* the language and the sounds being described *by* the language – what you may know as onomatopoeia. Sometimes the chains of sound are there largely for emphasis, to make an aggressive undercurrent in the poem feel more aggressive, a gentle or lyrical tone seem gentler and so on. And sometimes identical sounds proliferate simply because Hopkins is a very sensuous poet; strongly believing in the musical or aural element in poetry, the texture of the sound-world he creates is vital to him, and a constitutive element in any poetic sound-world, alongside distinctive rhythms, is clearly projected repetition of particular sound patterns.

The first thing is to look at the features of style identified above as key elements in the Hopkins sound-world.

Activity

Look again at the sonnets *God's Grandeur* (p. 15) and *Pied Beauty* (p. 19). Read both aloud, several times, concentrating on the octets. How many examples of alliteration and/or assonance can you detect? What initial ideas do you have about why Hopkins uses this technique here?

Discussion

Looking at the sonnet, *God's Grandeur* I can see examples of alliteration in phrases such as '**l**ike **sh**ining from **sh**ook foil' (2); '**r**eck his **r**od' (4); '**d**earest freshness **d**eep **d**own things' (10). There is a strong sense of assonance in 's**eared** with trade; bl**eared**', 'sm**eared** with toil' (6) and 'w**ears** man's smudge and sh**ares** man's smell' (7) (both of these examples also involve alliteration).

In *Pied Beauty*, an example of alliteration and assonance combined is couple-colour (2). A nice example of multiple alliteration is provided by '**L**andscape **pl**otted and **p**ieced **f**old, **f**allow, and **p**lough' (5). There is assonance in the echoing long vowels in 'r**o**se-m**o**les' (3) and in 'f**i**nches' w**i**ngs' (4).

Alongside this emphasis on successive consonant/vowel patterns, intricate chains of sounds develop throughout the poem; e.g. moving through lines 1–8, 'the chain da**ppl**ed' (1), 'cou**ple**' (2), 'sti**pple**' (3), '**pl**otted' (5), '**pl**ough' (5), 'tac**kle**' (6), 'fic**kle**, fre**ckle**d' (8), where I sense the liquid sound of the letter *l* is being deliberately exploited in a sequence of combinations, sometimes at the end of a word, sometimes at the beginning.

Sound and Sense

Assuming none of these patterns is accidental or random, what is the point? Both poems involve God and nature, the former as the all-powerful creator of the latter. Nature is felt to be beautiful, worthy of veneration in its own right. Hopkins draws attention to the features he wants to highlight, stresses them for attention in reading, by building up aural connections via simple repetitions within a phrase or line, or as in the last example through elaborate sound patterning over a longer scale. The meanings become more memorable through being embodied in a highly-composed framework of rhythm and sound. Scholars have linked this stress on alliteration and internal rhyme to the 'consonant chime' traditionally employed in Welsh poetry – 'Cynghanedd' (pronounced Kung-hanneth) – which Hopkins discovered during his period of study at St Beuno's College, North Wales, in the 1870s.

Links between sound and sense? Perhaps Hopkins links the features represented in the poem through common patterns of sound to suggest the idea that all things are ultimately related to each other as the work of a single creator. Assonance and alliteration, techniques for establishing 'kindredness' in word sound, might be for Hopkins useful tools for symbolizing the kindredness of all the elements making up the created world.

You may not be convinced by this line of argument; you may find it far-fetched or unnecessary. It assumes that sound patterns in a poem cannot be ends in themselves, but should be interpreted as playing a role in establishing themes; they are functional elements, contributing towards the complex of meaning represented by the poem. This may seem contrived, as if a poem is complex the way a clock is complex, with an involved hierarchy of parts and functions contributing towards one functional goal. The hypothesis suggested here may therefore seem to you over-concerned with finding an explanation for the sound patterns in these poems; sounds do not need a rational purpose or justification, poems are not machines. End of argument.

If you adopt this view, you might want to return to the sensuous interpretation of sound in Hopkins, a view earlier highlighted in the context of a poem's musical or aural dimension. If Hopkins frequently exploits the sounds of language in his poems it is because he finds them intrinsically interesting or pleasurable. Whichever approach you adopt: sounds as sensuous ends in themselves; sounds as functional elements within an organized complex of meaning; it seems clear that *sounds* are at least as important to Hopkins as is the *sense* of the words he employs. And it may be worth noting that whereas the developing interest in **sprung rhythm** first materializes in a specific text at a specific time, *The Wreck of the Deutschland*, composed in 1875–6, the feeling for sound in his writing is strongly embedded prior to that: you need only look at a poem already discussed in terms of its rhythmic qualities, *The Habit of Perfection* (p. 2), to see this.

As in later poems, there is plentiful alliteration, assonance and chiming: the effect of echoing, subtly altering syllabic patterns, the 'Cynghanedd' mentioned on page 110. In this area, its similarity to a later poem like *Hurrahing in Harvest* (p. 20) is probably greater than any marked differences. There is the evidence of phrases such as *Pipe me to pastures still* (2) or *Coils, keeps, and teases simple sight* (12). The stress on similar sound effects in *Hurrahing in Harvest* is immediately apparent; *barbarous in beauty* (1), *greeting of realer, of rounder replies* (8). What most distinguishes the two poems from each other is less sound than the context in which it is located; the **sprung rhythm** used in the later poem allows Hopkins to introduce urgencies and moments of special stress which are inevitably harder to achieve in a more regular metrical scheme. And the use of **sprung rhythm** to underline this dramatic conception of what happens in a poem is itself facilitated by the range of effects made possible through sound patterning.

Hearing versus Reading

You may already have seen from the Notes to several of the poems in this selection how seriously Hopkins thought about this musical dimension of his poems. On more than one occasion he argued with sceptical admirers that the underlying sense of a text which they regarded as over-complicated or difficult could be grasped just by listening to a good reading of the poem in question. In this connection, you might want to refer to the Notes to the poems *The Loss of the Eurydice* (p. 70), *Spelt from Sibyl's Leaves* (p. 90) and *Tom's Garland* (p. 93). The evidence is that Hopkins differentiated between the 'heard' experience of a text and the 'read' experience. And this would give weight to the 'sensuous' argument developed on p. 109; Hopkins wants to project a strongly-defined sound world in his poems. You might argue that the stress on sound and the innovative use of rhythm actually complement each other; the music in the poems sets out to be utterly distinctive, peculiar to its creator. It works with, but can be enjoyed separately from, the ideas which provide this music with its special themes.

Activity

The idea of a 'music' has been introduced. To develop this analysis a little more, please look at the octet of the sonnet '*As kingfishers catch fire*' (p. 16). There are five stresses to each line in the rhythm. Try putting these stresses into the lines, then read them, preferably several times; this is a good group activity! Note down some initial responses to links between sound and meaning in these eight lines. Then, look at the sound-commentary which follows.

Discussion

The opening line falls symmetrically into two parts, each involving multiple alliterations (*k* / *c*; *f* in the first half: *dr*, *fl* in the second). The semicolon at the end of the line emphasizes this sense of equal balance, by creating a strong endline pause, but the next line and a bit reads as a continuous phrase, with a strong alliterative effect through *r* sounds and a subtler thread picked out in the assonance chime *rim ... ring* (2–3). The predominance of single syllable words works with the five stress rhythm to produce a clipped, brisk effect as I read it. The most notable sound feature in the remainder of line 3 is the internal rhyme *tells ... bell's*, succeeded by strong alliteration on the *b* sound and another internal rhyme, this time sustained over three syllables: *hung ... swung ... tongue* (3–4). In addition, this sequence offers a half-rhyme echo of *ring* (3); and enforcing all of this, I have the feeling that Hopkins is establishing an onomatopoeic effect throughout lines 3–4, imitating through syllabic chimes the chiming sound of bells. By contrast, line 5 offers a break from sound decoration; it may even be that the unglamorous-sounding, prosaic *thing* used twice, may stress this switch from sensuous vocal score to something more mundane. In the following line, harder *d* sounds are softened by the liquid effect of *dwells* (6) as the endline rhyme word, while the initial stress in line 7 must be on the opening syllable, the coinage *Selves*, with the rest of the line dominated by this sibilant pattern of repeated *s* sounds (sibilants missing from only two words, *it* and *and*). The aural effect of the final line of the octet is determined by the repeated pronoun *I* (8), the sequence of strong, simple vowels – *do ... me ... for ... that ... came* (8) and the decisive mid-line pause of the colon. Indeed, any attempt to describe the aural qualities of these lines must take account of the punctuation. Colons or semicolons are used seven times in eight lines. You can add to that count the retarding effect of the hyphen in line 7. In reading these eight lines aloud, I am aware of a great richness and range in the opening quatrain (lines 1–4), offset by a plainer texture in lines 5–8. This seems a good point at which to end an aural analysis and begin investigating the sense of the lines.

The sophisticated sound technique highlighted in that last activity is *the* central and defining feature of Hopkins' style as a poet. To develop an understanding of the significance of the word 'style' here, it is not enough to say that his poems often describe things memorably. They do, but then so does the prose of his letters, diaries and journals – some of the finest prose of the Victorian era. In the poems, a musical dimension is introduced into the texture of the language through rhythmic stress patterns and elaborate sound sequences. The effect is to elevate the language beyond simple description and statement. Of course, you might say that all poets do this. You would be right; the point is that Hopkins accomplishes this through a highly personal idiom, characterized by rhythm as stress patterns and sound as chains, echoes and sequences. The poems are doing what all poems do, it is just that they do it in an unusual and distinctive way.

Binsey Poplars: Linking Sound and Sense

Before leaving the issue of style, it might be worth looking at a poem other than a sonnet, where formal links between octet and sestet are irrelevant, where the closely disciplined rhyme scheme of the sonnets can be relaxed. In addition, *Binsey Poplars* might offer some pointers when thinking about the themes in the poetry.

The approach followed here is simple; one reason for reading Hopkins is that his poems often suggest vivid descriptive powers enhanced by a musical feel for sound and rhythm. How well does this text display these qualities? And, more provocatively, if such qualities do exist in the poem, is that all there is to it – a succession of pleasant sounds and rhythms?

Activity

Looking at *Binsey Poplars* (p. 26), what do you notice about sound and rhythm?

Discussion

The rhythmical range, from two to six stresses per line, gives the poem a real sense of movement, an ebb and flow variation between longer and shorter verses. Repetition and internal rhyme figure throughout, helping enforce a feeling of 'interconnectedness' in the lyric; perhaps they are also used to underline its rhythmical character (see lines 3, 5, 16). Alliteration occurs extensively throughout, itself linked to this organic quality. From the repeated *qu* and *l* sounds in lines 1–2, to the proliferation of sibilants in the closing lines, it is clear that Hopkins is keen to score a sound-picture full of links and echoes.

Overall then, movement and variety in the rhythm, patterning in the sound structure. Can we jump from these stylistic traits, now identified across a range of texts, to the actual subject matter of the poem? Discussion so far has been concerned with the idiom, the voice. But what do we hear as that voice is communicating with us?

Approaches through Hopkins' Subjects

An entry in Hopkins' Journal for 8 April 1873 records the effect upon him of the felling of an ashtree:

> The ashtree growing in the corner of the garden was felled. It was lopped first: I heard the sound and looking out and seeing it maimed there came at that moment a great pang and I wished to die and not to see the inscapes of the world destroyed any more.

Binsey Poplars was written in response to an event nearly six years later (March 1879), but the thread of feeling connecting the two texts is obvious; by 1879 Hopkins was sufficiently accomplished a poet to channel his sense of grief and loss into an elegy, in the first instance for a line of trees by the Thames just west of Oxford, more generally though for all manifestations of natural beauty and order destroyed by human action.

Hopkins the Nature Poet

Every poem so far discussed has included a strong element of descriptive writing. The focus of that element each time has been Hopkins' sense of the beauty of nature. It seems right to consider Hopkins a true 'nature poet' in the sense that physical nature is never a mere backdrop in his poems, something picturesque brought in as decoration; instead, it is often at the heart of the experience Hopkins wishes to communicate.

Activity

Look at the three poems *Spring* (p. 16), *Inversnaid* (p. 31) and *Ribblesdale* (p. 34). Can you find any common threads in what the poems say about nature?

Discussion

All three poems focus on specifics; Hopkins' evocations of nature are never vague or in a wordy soft focus. In *Spring*, he peers so minutely at the birds' eggs that they *look little low heavens* (3), whilst the parent bird's piercing call is heard to *rinse and wring /The ear* (4–5). The highland stream observed in *Inversnaid* is visualized even to the froth formed on the surface of its pools (5–7), whilst the fierce motion of the stream moistens with water vapour *Wiry heathpacks, flitches of fern* (11), sensuous details caught in concise, alliterative phrasing. In the third poem, the lush Lancashire countryside is described *with leaves throng /And louched low grass* (1–2). Throughout, there is evidence of a feeling for particulars, the significance of observed details, and of course for sound clusters which stress these details. But the poems are not simply versified descriptions of places or seasons. In *Spring*, the first part of the sonnet does focus explicitly on the keen beauty of a time when nature is coming to life after the sterility of winter, but the sestet adopts a more urgent tone (see Notes p. 65) in directing attention to human beings. In *Inversnaid* three stanzas of physical description give way to a final stanza full of the same 'ecological' vision to be seen at work in *Binsey Poplars*. In *Ribblesdale*, even the octet seems more concerned with God than with nature; the following sestet is taken up with man as the most problematic aspect of the creation.

Nature and Religion

So the continued focus on nature, grounded in such specifics as the unique flight pattern of the kestrel, the call of the lark ascending beyond sight, the shade offered by a perfect line of riverside poplars, involves a set of values as well as the writer's descriptive powers. What principally distinguishes Hopkins' response to nature in this selection is his belief in its divine authorship.

This belief has already been touched on in the initial discussion of

The Windhover (see pp. 104–5). In that text, it can be argued that Hopkins sets up a complex and teasing relationship between the kestrel he observes and Christ. More generally throughout the poems in this selection, Hopkins celebrates nature as something inherently good, because created by a loving God, as inherently beautiful, its beauty also reflecting in physical forms the ideal beauty of the creator. An important conclusion follows from this. The beauty of the creation being our only sensory access to the beauty of the creator, we might be justified in seeing an element of prayer, of worship, in the way that the poems make so much of the poet's direct experience of nature. So that the frequency with which Hopkins celebrates nature itself directly reflects his intense religious beliefs; in conveying his response to the beauty observed in nature, Hopkins is revealing his attitude of reverence for the creative power sustaining physical nature.

This line of argument can be used to consolidate our sense of Hopkins as a 'nature poet'. He believes that the energies and vastness of nature require an order that is willed and consciously sustained. There is an ultimate purpose; nature is not something contingent, an accidental combination of molecules, a random set of phenomena that might have been different, or might not have been at all. In looking at Hopkins' ideas about nature, it is difficult if not impossible to ignore the element of awe, of respect and admiration directed towards some all-powerful creative force. It is used here in a deliberately vague sense; not religion as a set of dogmas, but as an intuitive belief in controlling forces beyond rational investigation.

Activity

Look at the lyric *Spring and Fall* (p. 30). In the light of the previous discussion, is there anything religious about the way Hopkins explores nature in the poem?

Discussion

In this poem I think Hopkins is using nature, not, as earlier mentioned, as a convenient backdrop, something pretty or decorative, but to say something about human experience. The easy but unpatronized grief of the child, experiencing natural decline and decay for the first time in the shape of autumn leaves, is symbolic of innocence. Her thoughts are *fresh* (4), her feelings spontaneous and touching. Hopkins imagines the older, more care-worn Margaret as blind to the natural sadness of autumn, yet weeping still; weeping for her own mortality and imperfection. The summing-up of the final rhyming couplet makes explicit the religious dimension at work; sin and death are the heavy realities provoking the older woman's sorrow, *It is Margaret you mourn for* (15). *Fall* is both autumn and the discovery of evil; for Hopkins this makes mankind the most problematic factor in the whole of nature.

Nature and Beauty: Inscape

Along with **sprung rhythm**, the other concept frequently associated with Hopkins is that of **inscape**. The word has already appeared in these Approaches. If you look back to the discussion of *Binsey Poplars* (p. 115), you will find the note from his Journal where Hopkins laments the felling of a tree, feeling he would die rather than *see the inscapes of the world destroyed any more*. The word never occurs in the poems in this selection, although it occurs frequently in the Journal and the ideas behind it influence many of the poems here. So what is **inscape**?

At its simplest, the word involves two linked ideas. The first is that all phenomena we can observe in nature possess some organizing secret which makes them what they are, which gives them the particular form of beauty they reveal to the observer. Prior to his coinage of the word, there are passages in the Journals where Hopkins is struggling to clarify his thinking; he worries about the organization of oak trees, desperate to find the uniquely distinctive pattern which is theirs. Then a few days later, a sense of Eureka!: *I have now found the law of the oak leaves...*(the Journal, July 1866). He finds this *law*, the key to the creator's secret in the oak tree, in the way its leaves are patterned. Hopkins has yet to find the word, but he now has the concept. **Inscape** is the underlying form, the essence, of an object; not the surface irregularities which make it one oak leaf rather than another, but the quality intrinsic to all oak leaves, what you might call their 'oak leaf-ness'. And what goes for oak leaves applies equally to kestrels, poplar trees, clouds, thrushes' eggs, ploughed fields, etc.

For Hopkins what is most real about things in the physical world is not to be found through casual observation; **inscape** is discovered through sudden, unexpected insight: the epiphany mentioned in connection with *The Windhover* on page 104. This concept of **inscape** as developed by Hopkins owes much to his preoccupation with philosophy, especially with metaphysics, the investigation of such abstract concepts as being, identity and time. In the writings of the medieval thinker Duns Scotus, Hopkins found a kindred spirit, who stressed the essence of each thing, beyond appearances, as its *haecceitas, thisness,* a concept very close to **inscape**.

But the **inscape** is not obvious or self-evident, which leads on to the second key element in the concept. While anyone with eyes can see the physical detail of the object, it requires vision to experience this sense of underlying form, the essence of the object. Another Journal entry in July 1872 describes in precise detail the interior of a barn, the *big bold A's* of the timber frames, after which Hopkins makes this regretful comment: *I thought how sadly beauty of inscape was unknown and buried away from simple people and yet how near at hand it was if they had eyes to see it.*

True apprehension of beauty depends on awareness of **inscape** since it is the **inscape** – the formal organizing and defining quality – which gives anything its intrinsic beauty. And linked closely to **inscape** is 'instress': the imaginative sensation experienced when an object's **inscape** is properly perceived. Only those whose vision goes beyond appearances experience the true beauty of natural phenomena; everyone else has only a glimmer, a weak reflection, of this beauty, like those who are tone-deaf or colour-blind.

Activity

Look again at the opening lines of the sonnet *God's Grandeur* (p. 15). Are there any links here with the ideas about **inscape** just discussed?

Discussion

If the account offered of **inscape** is valid, the opening three lines of this sonnet reveal Hopkins connecting the idea of the beauty experienced only when we sense the essence of something with the realization that this essence has been created by God. So a sense of natural beauty is connected directly with a religious sense of awe associated with the source of that natural beauty. But there is a problem here. If this *grandeur* (1) is seen to *flame out, like shining from shook foil* (2), is this not an image of something brilliant, vivid, unmistakable – like an electrical storm? There appears to be a contradiction: either the God-created **inscapes** are there for all to perceive and appreciate, or they are accessible only by the few with specially tuned spiritual or imaginative antennae. Which is it? Perhaps one answer to this puzzle is to say that Hopkins may not identify the beautiful exclusively with an object's **inscape**. Even surfaces may have elements of pattern or symmetry which contribute to an object's beauty. It may be that seeing even these lesser, surface patterns will lead people to connect them with the designing hand of God.

Inscape and the Voice

The aim here is to integrate points from the two discussions which have occupied this section of the Approaches. These two discussions have focused on Hopkins' style and on his concept of nature, this latter specifically linked to the idea of **inscape**. Most of the texts used to explore points so far have been sonnets, not least because of the central role the sonnet form plays in Hopkins' output, but here attention shifts to one of the longer poems in the selection, *The Leaden Echo and the Golden Echo* (p. 32).

The relevant Notes provide information on the circumstances in which the poem was written (see pp. 79–80). They draw attention to the antiphonal quality of the lyric, two opposed voices with opposed values. What immediately makes the poem relevant here is its concentration on beauty, shown most obviously by its 13 appearances in the text, mostly in repetitive clusters. The dialogue between the voices has a simple focus: a lament for the transience of physical beauty, counterpointed by a declaration of trust in an abiding (spiritual) source of undying beauty. The lament is *Leaden*, the grey appearance of fading, declining physical beauty; the contrary, upbeat tone is *Golden*, inherently precious and permanent.

Activity

Look at *The Leaden Echo* (p. 32); what features of the voice do you find here?

Discussion

This is probably best done after reading the text aloud, several times. I am aware of the **sprung rhythm** used, the huge swing between lines with a great rush of syllables and those with a single stress. There is a mass of alliteration and assonance (e.g. most of the opening line), a profusion of internal and end-rhymes, deliberate repetition (e.g. lines 13–16). Additionally, the macabre sequence of 'mortuary' images adds a ghoulish flavour to line 12. I think the cumulative effect of the rhythm, the repetitions and sound effects is meant to sound urgent, worried – the whole effect climaxing in the sixfold repetition of *despair* (15–16). But I can also see how for some readers the effects mentioned can seem forced, overdone; the musical connotations of the text may have led Hopkins to push effects handled elsewhere with finesse into a simplified, even garish form here. For those readers, the end result probably seems hectic and even melodramatic.

So much for the voice. In terms of its speech content, the key factor here is the contrast Hopkins draws between the transient beauties of the natural world and the immutable, eternal beauty of God. In particular, you have probably noticed that the natural beauty celebrated and mourned here is the beauty Hopkins finds in people rather than in other natural phenomena. A good text to look at if you wish to explore this aspect of Hopkins' outlook further is the sonnet *To what serves Mortal Beauty?* (see p. 40). The beauty of the individual flower lies ultimately in an **inscape** repeated in countless other flowers of the same kind; with human beings, it is less easy to come to terms with their mortality by arguing that the essential qualities for which we may love them or find them beautiful are inherent in all other human beings too. Instead the **inscapes** of the created beings mourned in *The Leaden Echo* are their eternal souls, and true experience of other souls must wait for our eternal lives after physical death.

Creators

For Hopkins, the beauty perceived as the intrinsic quality of each thing – its **inscape** – acts as a constantly repeated imaginative proof of the existence of a God who had created that **inscape** and was himself partly reflected in it. More than this, you could argue that when Hopkins wrote a poem, he was attempting through its form and language to reproduce the sense of **inscape** he found in the world around him. God was responsible for the (concealed) essence of each thing Hopkins saw; glimpsing this **inscape** reinforced Hopkins' sense of the beauty of the being who created it all; the poem then became an attempt to find words and rhythms capable of evoking for others the writer's sense of divine energy. This discussion has reached a point where consideration of style and ideas involves the relationship of two creators: Hopkins the creator of poetry and God the creator of everything celebrated in the poetry.

All of which leads on, inevitably, to a demanding group of texts where the eternal dramas of salvation matter to Hopkins even more than his deep feeling for the beauty of nature. Reading Hopkins involves all the factors explored so far in the Approaches, but it also involves something darker, arguably far less accessible. And what that might be is taken up in the following section.

Approaches through Hopkins' Religious Beliefs

Thy Terror, O Christ, O God

The image, so far: a voice, original, experimental, full of energetic rhythms and vivid language; preoccupied with the music of poetry, the aural effects of echo, rhyme, alliteration. The voice seems intoxicated with the freshness and variety of nature. It celebrates the creative energies alongside the created beauties; it projects a spring-time image of a world of enamelled perfection, created for our pleasure by an all-powerful God. This world is *charged with the grandeur of God* (p. 15 [1]); pregnant with *all this juice and all this joy* (p. 16 [9]). Indeed, when confronted by the full range of the creation,

All things, counter, original, spare, strange, (p. 19 [7]) Hopkins automatically reflects on its maker: *He fathers forth whose beauty is past change* (p. 19 [10]). It is no great surprise that the inevitable response is one of reverence and worship: *Praise him* (p. 19 [11]).

But this is a partial image. All is not sweetness and light. In the Christian understanding as Hopkins himself endorsed it, humanity came to the world as the apex of the creative enterprise, created in God's own likeness, but the free will which God allowed humans also allowed the possibility of sin. And with sin came transience, death, decay.

It is significant that even in one of the most celebratory of the 'nature' poems, the sonnet *Spring* (p. 16), the idyllic vision conveyed in the octet is described in the sestet as *A strain of the earth's sweet being in the beginning/In Eden garden.* (10–11). In regarding spring as a glimpse back into something irretrievably lost, the state of innocence and perfection which existed before sin brought death into nature, Hopkins reminds us that his sense of beauty is not something naïve or myopic, divorced from the darker realities of our human experience. So the aim of this final section is to provide some ideas about the religious foundations to Hopkins' awareness as a poet. You may agree with Hopkins' beliefs, you may violently disagree; you may be an agnostic unable to commit yourself for or against. You may yourself have a quite different set of beliefs. In an important sense, your attitude to the beliefs which underpin the poet's awareness is secondary; what matters is feeling some confidence about the shape of those beliefs, the effect they have on the writer's values and so the impact they have on the writing. The basic aim of this section is to provide suggestions for engaging with the religious perceptions at the heart of some of Hopkins' most demanding poems.

In the first instance, the focus needs to be biographical. It is hardly surprising that a religious strain runs through all the poems in this selection, from lyrics written as an undergraduate at Oxford in the mid 1860s through to sonnets composed a quarter century later, in the year of his death. The son of prosperous middle-class Victorian parents, themselves devout Anglicans, Hopkins was one of a considerable number of Oxford-educated Anglicans led by the influence and example of John Henry Newman to convert to Roman

Catholicism. Once converted, it was only two years before Hopkins started his training for the Jesuit ministry.

The ascetic qualities which had existed in Hopkins as an Anglican were to be even more rigorously enforced in his life as a priest. The Jesuit order had been established in direct response to the Protestant Reformation of the Sixteenth century; valuing intellectual as well as spiritual strengths in those who joined it, the order demanded formidable standards of effort and integrity. Prone to bouts of nervous illness, frail in his own physical constitution, the sense of beauty already discussed in these Approaches is perhaps all the more remarkable when one realizes the spiritual and emotional pressures which religious belief often caused Hopkins. Whatever one thinks about his religion, the evidence of the poems is that it can never be dismissed as simplistic, blind to doubts or relentlessly optimistic. Indeed, this discussion may leave you with the feeling that it can indeed be the opposite of all three: intellectually strenuous, hesitant and often comfortless.

The Theological Context: Original Sin

For Hopkins, the original sin which all humanity has inherited from Adam leaves us sinful and liable to punishment from God as the perfect embodiment of justice. But as a Christian, Hopkins also believes that we can be spared this deserved punishment through divine mercy, since God is also the perfect embodiment of love. So the sense of God disclosed in his poems involves a delicate balancing act. Hopkins reveres the loving God and trembles in the presence of the just God. This is a classically Christian dialectic, balancing of opposed or contradictory concepts; the individual, sensitive to his condition, hoping for an undeserved eternity in paradise from the loving God, fearful of a wholly deserved eternity in Hell from the cosmic judge. It is this dramatic spiritual context which gives us the key to the darkest in mood of all Hopkins' poems, the so-called 'Sonnets of Desolation', written towards the end of his life and the longest of his poems, *The Wreck of the Deutschland*.

Activity

Look at the opening stanza of *The Wreck of the Deutschland* (p. 3). How similar in technique is it to other texts already discussed? What might you say of the characterization of God in the stanza?

Discussion

The **sprung rhythm** is evident at once. Stresses vary between two (in the first line of the stanza) and six (in the final line). In *Part the first* this gives a stress sequence in each stanza of 2,3,4,3,5,5,4,6. In this opening stanza stresses often fall on single syllable words (*Thou* (1), *me* (1) *breath* (2), *bread* (2)); the effect is to make the rhythm feel energetic. But the energy seems anxious; God, *mastering* (1), is responsible for life, making the poet who he is, but he almost *unmade* (6) him too. The emphatic alliteration contributes both to the urgent rhythm and to the feeling of unease. This quality may also perhaps relate to the use of rhyme; the way three rhymes are used in each eight line stanza (ababcbca) means that strong sounds at the start of each stanza recur at the end, suggesting the effect of constraint or limitation. The impression offered in this stanza of the poet's attitude to God is probably best revealed by the final word of line 6, *dread*. There is an awareness of obligation to God, alongside an overwhelming impression of divine power. But the idea of divine love is totally absent.

The Wreck of the Deutschland: Celebrating Providence

The poem offers you both challenge and pleasure. The challenge comes from those passages where Hopkins wishes to articulate complex religious meanings via an idiom whose originality can work against immediate understanding. But the pleasure comes from those areas of the poem where that same idiom is matched with an appropriate content, and the result is the same lyrical fluency identified as a distinctive strength in other poems.

Above all, it is an ambitious poem: in its 280 lines Hopkins can be seen using a particular event as a symbol for a theme he regarded as universal: Christ's redemptive love for sinful, undeserving humanity. In the shorter poems you can see how an underlying theme is disclosed through something concrete and specific: think of *The*

125

Windhover, Binsey Poplars, Hurrahing in Harvest. In each case, reflection on the **inscape** of a natural object or scene triggers in Hopkins' imagination some religious insight about the reality underpinning the world of appearances. You can apply the same criterion to other poems in this selection; indeed you might find it interesting to use this as an approach to the poems, judging for yourself how valuable a factor it proves when trying to make overall sense of your response to Hopkins.

The point here is that Hopkins does not choose an object or scene as the starting point for his poem. Instead, he is inspired by an event; a disaster, a shipwreck involving heavy loss of life. The disaster in turn prompts thoughts about the nature of God's relationship to mankind; thoughts about providence; thoughts about martyrdom; thoughts about the link between human suffering and Christ's suffering. This all makes the conceptual focus of the poem demanding on its readers, since Hopkins assumes a readership knowledgeable about the theological elements of the text (it was originally submitted for publication in the Jesuit magazine *The Month* and rejected as too difficult.) And it must be said that reading is made still more demanding at times by the voice. The tone may be urgent and innovative, but the stressful rhythmic patterns require economy of language, and when this economy is accompanied by coinages and wordplay, the act of reading can sometimes become a painstaking process of sorting clues.

Activity

Read stanza 27 (p. 12) again, more than once, and if possible aloud. Try to catch the sequence of stress patterns indicated on page 125. If you write the stanza out as prose, keeping Hopkins' original words and punctuation, is the meaning made any easier to grasp? What points in the stanza would you single out as causing particular problems?

Discussion

As prose, keeping to Hopkins' words and punctuation but disregarding line breaks, I am struck by the unnatural run of clauses broken up by the heavy punctuation of lines 210–13:

> The jading and jar of the cart,
> Time's tasking, it is fathers that asking for ease
> Of the sodden-with-its sorrowing heart,
> Not danger, electrical horror;

If the *jading and jar* (210) is described as *Time's tasking* (211), it is in syntactical terms in apposition to this second phrase, which is the subject of the verb *fathers* (211); so at the start, a 'proper' prose version might read 'It is the jading and jar of the cart, time's tasking, which fathers that asking for ease of. . .' Putting the stanza into prose only highlights the inversions and reversals of customary order which feature in Hopkins' poetic syntax. But the distortion of the expected order is responsible for only part of the interpretative challenge here. For the full sense of the clauses ending at the line 213 semicolon to emerge, you have to hold line 210 in your head until *Not danger, electrical horror;* (213) since the whole sequence stands on the relation *Time's tasking* (211). . . *fathers* (211). . . *Not danger* (213), a vital contrast, explaining that the nun's anguish is the consequence of a long term spiritual attrition (*Time's tasking* [211]), not the response to the critical situation she finds herself in. So Hopkins' syntax, his approach to the order and sequence of clauses and words, is a possible source of challenge as you read. Here is a simple example of this: I can say that on my own first attempt to make sense of line 211 I was thwarted by the words *it is fathers*, since I read *fathers* as a plural noun rather than a crucially weighted verb! But syntax is not the only hurdle we meet here. The richly alliterative *sodden-with-its sorrowing heart* (212) needs unpacking; the nun's heart is 'wet' with sorrow, the implied metaphor that of tears. *Electrical horror* (213) offers a strong example of Hopkins' taste for the flamboyant, new-minted phrase, but I suspect it is there largely to add some local colour to the otherwise rather naked *danger* (213), and it strikes a curious note – why electrical? There are some potential problems too in the final couplet; partly syntactic (the disjointed clause order), partly the consequence of compactness, the omission of everyday words like 'is' and 'the'. That said, the surging alliteration of line 216 gives a powerful sense of the poem's intermittent storm music through the six stressed accents (*Burden. . . wind's. . . burly. . . endragonèd seas*), whilst that final image of the *endragonèd seas* (216) compensates for much of the preceding obscurity.

Inscape and Structure

In exploring an event here rather than an object or scene, Hopkins is taking on a subject inherently more dynamic and so stronger in dramatic potential. The claim was made on page 122 that Hopkins is attempting in each of his poems to articulate the **inscape** of its subject. If that claim is valid, what can be said about **inscape** in relation to *The Wreck of the Deutschland*?

A start might be made by examining structure. The poem is structured in two unequal parts, the first in ten eight line stanzas, the second in 25 stanzas. There is an immediate and important contrast between the parts: in *Part the first*, we have a sense of the writer's spiritual life and his paradoxical, all-embracing sense of God. The section ends with two stanzas composed like a prayer, where Hopkins returns to the tone of the beginning, a pious believer's anxious address to God. There is violence and energy in the rhythms and language of *Part the first*, but they seem to be provoked by something private and intimate: the poet's own relationship to God.

By contrast, *Part the second* takes us straight to the situation referred to in the poem's title, something dramatic in the physical world, an event involving terror, distress, loss of life. It is a December night. A ship sailing from Germany to the United States loses its bearing and is grounded on a sandbank in the Thames estuary off the Essex coast. Conditions are appalling; high seas, snow driven on an east-north-easterly gale. Amongst the passengers are five German nuns, driven to find exile in the United States by the harsh anti-Catholic laws established by German chancellor Bismarck and implemented by his minister Falck (hence the reference in the poem's dedication). Of the two hundred plus passengers on board, over a quarter are drowned, including the nuns. One is reported to have cried out 'O Christ, come quickly!' (see stanza 24, p. 11) before succumbing to exhaustion and dying in the icy North Sea waters. So, what about **inscape**?

Here is one possibility, one approach. *Part the second* narrates the fate of the ship and those on board, but it is in no respect simply a narrative – a fact of which you are probably already well aware. Indeed, Hopkins was at pains to make clear his own view that the whole poem is not a narrative but an ode: a poem taking a place, person or event as the initial stimulus for a process of reflection. In a letter to Robert Bridges, dated 2 April 1878, Hopkins confessed that The Deutschland *would be more generally interesting if there were more wreck and less discourse, I know, but it is still an ode and not primarily a narrative*. The need here is to integrate the narrative elements in the poem, generally recognizable by their greater immediacy or impact, into Hopkins' larger design. You might pick out in this context stanzas 11–17, 19, 24. The **inscape** may start from narration of an event, but it also needs to refer to the reflective portions of the text, what Hopkins calls in his letter the *discourse*.

For Hopkins as he reflected, the event presented a mystery, a religious difficulty. The nuns, already persecuted in Germany, meet a terrible death on board the intended means of their escape. A black irony? Fate playing a cruel hand? For Hopkins, Fate, blind destiny, was part of the mythological apparatus of paganism, of Greek tragedy. Instead, as a Christian, his own faith was centred on what stanza 31 calls *lovely-felicitous Providence* (245). But what is so lovely about a design for the world which allows five women who have dedicated their lives to the service of God, just as Hopkins did himself, to suffer the agonies of death by shipwreck?

Activity

Look up the word *felicitous* (245) in a dictionary. If you need to, check also on the meaning of *Providence* (245). How might the ideas in the words be linked?

Discussion

As noted above, the original sense of 'felicitous' is blissful, happy. The word can however involve two other senses: apt or appropriate, and ingenious, clever. If 'Providence' involves the concept of God's care ('providing') for his creation, his designer's careful concern, you have in the two words the notion of a design, a plan, either apt or clever or both. Clever plans are often plans which contain much more than you see at first. The divine plan for humans is *lovely* (245) but also clever, appropriate – appropriate for humans who are sinners, who have a right only to punishment? The more you look at the phrase, the more you may come to feel it is saying something at the heart of Hopkins' perceptions in this poem.

Inscape, Design, Providence: 'Lightning and Love'

The poet who composed *The Wreck of the Deutschland* accepts that there is a problem in reconciling divine love and divine power. The event provoking the poem seems to demonstrate far more of the latter than of the former. But Hopkins' faith turns a problem into a mystery, a sense of the ultimate goodness of the divine plan which cannot be explained or justified on wholly rational grounds. What the entire text might be seen as encapsulating then is the believer's sense of that mystery; the **inscape** Hopkins wants to evoke throughout the poem is his deep intuition that pain and death finally make sense in, are not contradictions of, a universe created and sustained by a loving God.

Within his contradictory experience of God, Hopkins' faith tells him that *Providence* is *lovely-felicitous* (245), despite contrary appearances. But this cannot be demonstrated logically, there are no rational proofs; the **inscape** discovered in the loss of the ship is the creative good that underpins even such seeming evils as suffering and loss of innocent life. The prayerful tone at the end of stanza 9 (p. 6) offers one clue, itself full of paradoxical ideas, to this suggested **inscape**:

> Beyond saying sweet, past telling of tongue,
> Thou art lightning and love, I found it, a winter and warm;
> Father and fondler of heart thou has wrung;
> Hast thy dark descending and most art merciful then.

69–72

If the feeling here is linked to the thought developed towards the end of the poem, particularly in stanzas 32–3, this explanation of the poem's underlying purpose – as the disclosure by Hopkins of the **inscape** of divine providence he has painfully glimpsed in the wreck of the ship – may start to make more sense. It is by no means the only way of reading and responding to the text, but it does allow you to think about linking narrative and reflective elements. It also offers a bridge between Hopkins' concerns and technique in this poem and those already examined in some of the sonnets and shorter poems.

The 'Sonnets of Desolation': Voicing Despair

In a sequence of sonnets written appproximately a decade after *The Wreck of the Deutschland*, Hopkins can be seen looking urgently for another kind of **inscape**, attempting to make sense of his own spiritual suffering. The exhilarating prayerful tones with which stanza 35 concludes that poem in celebratory style have disappeared; here the poet's own pain is the inescapable subject, and it is an experience where he finds little sense of divine consolation, no trace of *lovely-felicitous Providence* (p. 13 [245]).

Activity

Look again at the sonnets '*No worst*', (p. 40) and '*I wake and feel*' (p. 39). Concentrate particularly on the sestets, lines 9–14. What can you say about tone in these lines, and do you find any links between tone and technique here?

Discussion

The emotional landscape of both poems is dark and threatening. In each case the octet dramatizes the poet's extreme mental distress, whilst the sestet seems to take a tentative step back, offering an instant of reflection. In '*No worst*', Hopkins conveys something of the horrors of isolation, picturing himself dizzy with vertigo in an 'alpine' mental landscape. What small relief he finds is bleakness itself; there is at least the nightly oblivion of sleep and the final oblivion of death. And in '*I wake and feel*', this sobriety is mixed with a caustic dose of self-disgust; he loathes himself, identifying this powerful self-loathing (itself suicidal in tone?) with divine punishment. In this sestet the use of the personal pronoun (*I, me*) emphasizes the sense of isolation. Hell defined not as 'other people' (as the French writer J.P. Sartre expressed it) but as oneself, the mind left alone to contemplate its own inadequacy and failure. In both poems I notice in particular the absence of the playful element in earlier texts: the proliferation of inventions, compounds and sound chimes. The tone is severe, the technique appropriately disciplined and channelled to mirror this.

Why this black tone? If these are the poems *written in blood* to which Hopkins made a tantalizing reference in a letter to Bridges of May 1885, what can explain the mood change from earlier texts to this sequence of poems variously described by later commentators as 'the Sonnets of Desolation', 'the terrible sonnets' or 'the dark sonnets'? A possible explanation is offered quite explicitly in one of these texts (see Notes to '*To seem the stranger*' p. 83).

Do the language, syntax and rhythms employed in these poems help you to feel the sense of despair experienced by the *I* of the poems? Or do they instead give you a feeling of artifice, of something posed, melodramatic, an exercise in conveying extreme states of dejection? And what part might the voice explored earlier have in this? If the playful elements are conspicuously absent (see Discussion, p. 131), what remains is the compactness or economy of style, the tense syntax, which so often operates as an infallible voice print in Hopkins.

Activity

Look at the octet of the sonnet (*Carrion Comfort*) (p. 41). How far might it be seen to bear out the critical points made in the last sentence above?

Discussion

The suggestion is that in these late sonnets one ingredient of the voice – the fondness for sound play, echo chains – has largely vanished; what remains characteristic is the compact syntax, the 'jumps' in sense which the reader needs to make in establishing meaning in the text.

In these eight lines there is still evidence of sound play, interest in the sensuous aural pleasure of sound clusters – a consistent trait in Hopkins. Look for instance at the vigorously alliterative sequence in line 6 with *r* and *l* sounds uppermost in the pattern. Similar alliterative patterns occur in the following lines, whilst assonantal rhyme (vowel sounds) is used internally in the *me. . .me. . .thee. . .flee* sequence of line 8; all quite consistent with the account already offered of the vocal qualities in Hopkins' earlier poems (see p. 109–15). But now the music seems less exuberant and more intense; the six stresses per line of the **sprung rhythm** create a longer, more emphatic effect. This heavier stress pattern is particularly noticeable in lines 1–4, where the sequence of repeated negatives helps to reinforce a feeling of struggle, of grim determination to hang on.

The syntax of these first four lines is direct; there is little of the sense jumping or strange ordering of clauses which occurs in lines 5–8. Here, the syntax offers me a disconnected phrase order needing repeated readings for the underlying sense to emerge. Think about the placing of the adverb *rude* in line 5, or the sense of the words *me frantic* in the second half of line 8. What earlier phrases do you need to keep in mind to make sense of the interrogative *lay a lionlimb against me?* in line 6? All of these examples highlight features of the voice which result from a powerful need in Hopkins to create stylistic originality and distinctiveness through economy, omission, exaggerated attention to non-standard word order (the syntax issue). Hence, cumulatively, the idea of the unique voice print.

The Voice, its Themes and its Range

Earlier poems in the selection have celebrated the natural world in a way special to Hopkins, but within a long tradition of lyric poetry where lightly-stressed rhythms combine with vividly descriptive sounds and imagery to evoke a sense of the writer's joyful encounters with nature. Like the creator God of *Genesis*, the lyrical Hopkins surveyed the beauty of nature and *saw that it was good* (*Genesis* 1,10). Such poems as *Pied Beauty* (p. 19), *God's Grandeur* (p. 15) *Spring* (p. 16) and perhaps most of all, *The Windhover* (p. 18), provide compelling evidence for this point of view.

With *The Wreck of the Deutschland* (p. 3) another dimension is introduced; within the acknowledged beauty of nature, there is a constant dynamic, growth and decay, birth and death, creation and destruction. And for Hopkins, the drama of humanity is at the centre of this universal dynamic: humanity as the creation so loved by the creator that he sacrificed part of himself to give it a chance of paradise. Encompassing both good and evil, light and dark, the sense of nature in these texts is celebratory; throughout, you can argue that light triumphs in the grand design planned and executed by a loving creator. So lyrical and dramatic elements combine in *The Wreck of the Deutschland* to offer an upbeat vision where human suffering and death are justified by an ultimately confident faith.

But in these later sonnets just discussed, that upbeat vision is absent. There is a strong element of drama: Hopkins articulates feelings of hurt and loss, he is the rejected lover. Unable to accept estrangement from his beloved, he cannot reconcile himself to a life devoid of meaning or purpose. He feels suicidal; he talks of his *sad self* (2), his *tormented mind* (3), (see the sonnet 'My own heart', p. 42). If it makes any sense to talk of **inscape** in this context, then what the poems focus on is that underlying emotional reality of pain which results when the writer feels his relationship with God no longer inspires or animates him. Whether you regard the factors giving rise to these sonnets as spiritual crisis or nervous collapse (or both) is irrelevant; they expand our sense of Hopkins the poet, offering graphic images of emotional and psychological distress to set against those joyful, exultant **inscapes** of physical nature through which Hopkins first discovered his distinct voice. It turns out to be a voice capable of a far wider emotional range than might be suggested from a first, cursory look at his two earlier nature sonnets *Pied Beauty* (p. 19) or *Spring* (p. 16).

Conclusion

Hopkins was not a professional writer, in the sense that a professional writer earns his living from having his work published. He was a Catholic priest, a Jesuit, who died prematurely from complications after an attack of typhoid at the age of 45, having exhausted himself through a gruelling vocation of parish work and teaching for which in many ways he was not well-equipped. His poems were known only to a small number of admirers, one of whom, the poet Robert Bridges, collected, edited and published a number of them in 1918, nearly thirty years after Hopkins' death. His reputation as a poet is thus almost wholly posthumous. Even the friends who read drafts and final versions of the poems in manuscript often puzzled over Hopkins' meanings. Indeed, the editor who first brought the poetry to a wider audience expressed doubt over aspects of the writing; much of Bridges' regard for his friend's achievement was highly qualified, and it is likely that he would have been amazed by the enthusiasm which many readers have since felt for these poems. So Hopkins represents an interesting literary phenomenon: a Victorian poet who only finds a wide and appreciative readership some decades into the Twentieth century.

Bridges on Hopkins

The tone in which Robert Bridges writes of his late friend's poems is distinctly apologetic and defensive. He talks in an Introduction to Hopkins' poems of his *natural eccentricity*, defined as *a love for subtlety and uncommonness*. It is just possible that you may regard these qualities as virtues or strengths in a writer; Bridges did not, using the emotive word *injured* to describe the effect he felt such characteristics had on Hopkins' poetry. Elsewhere, he returns to this notion of *oddness* in Hopkins, with the comment that *it was an idiosyncrasy of this student's mind to push everything to its logical extreme, and take pleasure in a paradoxical result.*

Interestingly, Hopkins himself had commented to Bridges in a letter of 1879:

No doubt my poetry errs on the side of oddness. . . But as air, melody, is what strikes me most of all in music and design in painting, so design, pattern or what I am in the habit of calling inscape is what I above all aim at in poetry. Now it is the virtue of design, pattern or inscape to be distinctive and it is the vice of distinctiveness to become queer. This vice I cannot have escaped.

Bridges' suggestion seems to be that finding pleasure in paradoxes is somehow immoral, or at least not respectable. But what about the argument that paradox (a statement or idea which seems to involve violent contradictions) is at the heart of Hopkins' view of the world, particularly as depicted in *The Wreck of the Deutschland*? Significantly, it is Bridges who refers famously to this poem in his Preface to the 1918 first edition as *the great dragon coiled in the gate to forbid entrance*, as if it were something obviously daunting or inhibiting for potential readers.

He then itemizes the stylistic lapses identified in Hopkins' technique. These include everything from deliberate omission of the relative pronoun ('that'/'which') to bad rhymes and ambiguous homophones. The manner is reminiscent of an old-fashioned teacher censuring a wayward student's writing (the features just mentioned are described as *definite faults of style*). His reservations are not confined to style and grammar, however. In looking at *The Blessed Virgin compared to the Air we Breathe*, he criticizes its *exaggerated Marianism* (see Notes on pp. 81–3). He refers disparagingly to *the naked encounter of sensualism and asceticism which hurts The Leaden Echo and The Golden Echo*. Notice *hurts*; like *injured* quoted in the last paragraph the word suggests painful damage, a living organism affected by its creator's defects in matters of style and judgement. (Other ways of reading Hopkins' concerns in that text are suggested both in the Notes pp. 79–80 and on pp. 120–1 of the Approaches.) In reflecting on those alternative approaches, it may be hard to avoid the conclusion that at least part of Bridges' unease was over a poetry in which ideas were projected in a strong and uncompromising fashion.

When such negative points are set in a context where Bridges still wishes to highlight the beauty and insights he finds in Hopkins' poetry, we have an overall assessment which is, to say the least, mixed: the admiration is both qualified and puzzled. Bridges talks of the poems as if the appropriate criteria for response were those of polite manners or etiquette; there is a revealing comment in his Preface that Hopkins' style involves *a neglect of those canons of taste which seem common to all poetry*. Hopkins displays indifference to the implicit ideal of simplicity. The mannered, wilfully inventive idiom thereby not only qualifies any chance Hopkins has of becoming a 'classic' in the English literary canon; it is also an affront, intended or otherwise, to poetic decency. Indifferent to simplicity, Hopkins cultivates ambiguity, a quality Bridges by implication regards as deviant or improper.

That Hopkins has since made his way into that canon might be used to show how wrong Bridges was. But that would be a simplistic conclusion to draw, and it is certainly not the reason that Bridges has been introduced to this discussion. For one thing, the obligation which every reader (and editor) owes to Bridges' preservation and publication of the poems is immeasurable. However diffident the endorsement, it is surely right to maintain that Hopkins' reputation starts from the fact of that 1918 edition. Another factor is more significant still. Many of the features which Bridges highlights as technical or stylistic lapses in Hopkins, errors of taste, *are* present in the poems. What probably most divides later readers from Bridges' assessment is the evaluation of those agreed features.

Bridges saw much of Hopkins' stylistic originality as idiosyncratic, differing radically and unacceptably from tradition. Later readers have seen this quality in Hopkins as the essence of his achievement, what makes reading him a special and worthwhile experience. For Bridges and other Victorian readers, Hopkins failed to keep the right balance between innovation and tradition. Readers have since listened to the poet's voice explored in these Approaches as something daring and intense; a voice singing a new music which conveys insights about the **inscapes** of physical nature, religious experience, the relation of creator to creation.

The case against Hopkins is simple. The idiom can seem contrived, over-fussy, with an aristocratic disregard for the everyday rules of English syntax. Only the most partisan reader would pretend that *The Loss of the Eurydice* is not handicapped by stylistic exaggeration, or that the syntactical labyrinths of *Tom's Garland* or *Harry Ploughman* are always justified by the imaginative discoveries a reader is likely to bring back from her wanderings in them.

In Defence of Hopkins

Hopkins is one of the very few genuinely original poet-experimenters in English, with an idiom wholly and unmistakably his own. He is a writer in whom to a very marked degree inventive technique is matched by inventive thought. He is original, and complex, because he has original and complex things to say, and he is driven to formulate what he says in a style complementing the vision behind it. The argument is that Hopkins is a visionary. Like all visionaries, his art offers a challenging mixture of images immediately felt to be important alongside a boldness of technique that forces us to read on his terms rather than our own. The results in this selection can certainly be described as uneven; you may perhaps agree with Bridges that perfect integration of voice, form and theme happens quite rarely in the poems, yet the unevenness of the achievement should not be used to diminish its scale in those texts where the voice and its message are in harmony.

Reading Hopkins then is not easy because it is not *meant* to be easy – but it can be a moving and exhilarating experience. There is the sense of a mind intoxicated by nature and the creator behind it, for Hopkins more beautifully alive even than nature itself. With such great themes to develop, it is no surprise that this voice can sometimes pose problems in reading. Yet however angular or elliptical the syntax may become, the abiding core is the compelling sense of **inscape**: the formative beauty within all created things, above all in human beings. For Hopkins, we humans are the chief paradox of nature: body yet soul, mortal yet immortal, sinners yet made in the image of God. That vision of our own complex and bewildering **inscape** is realized most powerfully at the close of one of his finest and most characteristic poems, a sonnet which extends sonnet form far beyond the traditional parameters as Bridges and his contemporaries would understand them. With its sense of drama, its rhythmic energy and its alliterative music, the climax of *That Nature is a Heraclitean Fire and of the comfort of the Resurrection* (p. 46) seems a wholly apt point at which to end these Approaches and send you off again on your own further explorations. Bon voyage.

In a flash, at a trumpet crash,
I am all at once what Christ is, since he was what I am, and
This Jack, joke, poor potsherd, patch, matchwood, immortal
    diamond,
Is immortal diamond.

                          (21–4)

Chronology

1844   Hopkins born, 28 July, at Stratford in Essex. Comfortable middle-class Anglican background; father a marine insurance adjuster and prolific amateur writer

1845   Irish potato famine. John Henry Newman converts to Roman Catholicism, causing crisis in Anglican communion

1847   Charlotte Brontë, *Jane Eyre*; Emily Brontë, *Wuthering Heights*

1848   Marx and Engels, *The Communist Manifesto*

1850   Tennyson, *In Memoriam*; Catholic hierarchy restored in England

1854   Family having moved to Hampstead, Hopkins attends Highgate School

1859   Darwin, *On the Origin of Species*; J.S. Mill, *On Liberty*

1861   American Civil War; Dickens, *Great Expectations*

1863   Enters Balliol College, Oxford

1864   John Henry Newman's spiritual autobiography, *Apologia pro vita sua*

1866   Becomes a Catholic, to the great concern of his family; received into Catholic communion by John Henry Newman

1867   Graduates from Oxford with first class honours; teaches for eight months at Newman's Oratory School in Birmingham; *Teaching is very burdensome, especially when you have much of it: I have*; Disraeli's Second Reform Bill expands electorate; Fenian uprising in Ireland

1868   Resolves to become a Catholic priest, although aware of *great grief* this will cause his mother; burns the poems he has already composed (probable explanation for *murder of the innocents* reference in his Journal); begins training for the Jesuit priesthood

1869   Arnold, *Culture and Anarchy*

1870   Forster's Education Act establishes minimum state provision for schooling

1871 Test Act allows non-Anglicans to attend Oxford and Cambridge

1872 Discovers the work of Duns Scotus: *from this time I was flush with a new enthusiasm*

1874 As part of his training, goes to St Beuno's College; Hardy, *Far from the Madding Crowd*

1875 First serious attempt at poetry for seven years

1878 Sent to Stonyhurst College, Lancs., principal Jesuit school and training college; December, to Oxford as curate of parish church

1880 Posting to poor Liverpool parish of St Francis Xavier

1881 Henry James, *Portrait of a Lady*

1882 Returns to Stonyhurst to teach classics; British officials assassinated, Phoenix Park, Dublin; continued unrest against British rule

1884 Last major posting as professor of Greek and Latin literature at University College, Dublin

1886 Gladstone's Irish Home Rule Bill defeated in Commons; he resigns

1887 Queen Victoria's Golden Jubilee

1889 Starts year with spiritual retreat; contracts typhoid; dies, 8 June

1918 First edition of Hopkins' poems published by Oxford University Press and edited by Robert Bridges

Further Reading

Editions

There are two editions of Hopkins' complete poems available in paperback. The first has been the standard edition of the poems for many years:

W.H. Gardner and N.H. Mackenzie (ed.) *The Poems of Gerard Manley Hopkins* (Oxford University Press, 4th ed. 1970)

Catherine Phillips (ed.), *Gerard Manley Hopkins* (Oxford Authors Series, Oxford University Press, 1986)

Not yet in paperback is this scholarly edition of the poems (with variants):

N.H. Mackenzie (ed.), *Poems of Gerard Manley Hopkins* (Oxford University Press 1990).

Prose Writings

Hopkins' prose writings are worth study in their own right, and are certainly as readable and as stylish in their own way as the poems. They will add to your sense of Hopkins' personality and outlook, enriching your impression of the mind at work in the poems. The standard edition of Hopkins' letters is in three volumes and in hardback only:

C.C. Abbott (ed.), *Vol. I: The Letters of Gerard Manley Hopkins to Robert Bridges*; *Vol. II: The Correspondence of Gerard Manley Hopkins with R. W. Dixon*; *Vol. III: The Further Letters of Gerard Manley Hopkins* (Oxford University Press, 2nd ed. 1955–6).

There is also an attractive selection of letters in paperback which forms part of the Oxford Letters and Memoirs Series:

Catherine Phillips (ed.), *Gerard Manley Hopkins Selected Letters* (Oxford University Press, 1991).

The standard edition of Hopkins' Journals and Papers, which complements the more informal tone of the letters is again only available in hardback and is probably best sought out in libraries:

H. House and G. Storey (ed.), *The Journals and Papers of Gerard Manley Hopkins* (Oxford Unversity Press, 1959).

If you are interested in the religious dimensions of Hopkins' thinking, you will discover many absorbing reflections and insights in the following (again, only in hardback):

C. Devlin (ed.), *Sermons and Devotional Writings* (Oxford University Press, 1959).

Biography

Hopkins' life, particularly the impact on his creative development of his work as a Jesuit, is covered by this very readable biography in paperback.

Robert Bernard Martin, *Gerard Manley Hopkins – A Very Private Life* (Harper Collins, 1992).

Criticism

In terms of critical writing on the poetry, posterity has certainly made up for the sluggishness with which Hopkins first became known to a wide audience. In the following selection, you will find responses to qualities in the poetry which should stimulate your own thinking.

First, two helpful collections of essays, each in paperback, each with an introduction which helps throw light on the ways critical assessments of Hopkins have evolved over the past half century:

M. Bottrall (ed.), *Gerard Manley Hopkins: Poems* (Casebook series, Macmillan, 1975).

G. Hartman (ed.), *Hopkins: A Collection of Critical Essays* (Twentieth Century View Series, Prentice Hall, 1966).

The following longer studies of the poetry can be recommended:
G. Storey, *A Preface to Hopkins* (Longman, 1978).

N.H. MacKenzie, *A Reader's Guide to Hopkins* (Thames and Hudson, 1981).

J.R. Watson, *The Poetry of Gerard Manley Hopkins: A Critical Study* (Penguin Masterstudies Series, Penguin, 1987).

The single most influential essay on Hopkins, in terms of its impact on Hopkins' status and in terms of the insight it conveys on the poetry, is probably the chapter devoted to Hopkins in *New Bearings in English Literature* by F.R. Leavis. This was first published by Chatto and Windus in 1932, but has been reprinted in paperback by Penguin frequently since then. It is particularly interesting to read Leavis in the light of Robert Bridges' careful reservations on his late friend's genius.

Robert Bridges' reservations about Hopkins poetry are cogently developed by the independently-minded American critic, Yvor Winters in a section of his book:

Yvor Winters, *The Function of Criticism* (reprinted in the Hartman critical anthology mentioned above).

The following websites provide a wide range of critical, bibliographical and textual materials on Hopkins, with further links to sites exploring such key elements as his place within Victorian literature, his spirituality and the influence of his Jesuit vocation:

http://www.dundee.ac.uk/english/hopkins.htm

http://www.stg.brown.edu/projects/hypertext/landow/victorian/hopkins/gmhov.html

http://www.creighton.edu/-dcallon/Hopkins

http://www.literaryhistory.com/19thC/HOPKINS.htm

Tasks

1 Select three or four sonnets from this selection. How far do you consider they show Hopkins' versatility in writing sonnets? Does Hopkins avoid the risk of making the form monotonous? If so, how?

2 'The strongest feature of Hopkins' poetry is his vivid sense of nature.' Using evidence from the texts, discuss how useful – or how limiting – you find thinking about Hopkins as a 'nature poet'.

3 One feature of Hopkins' thought is his preoccupation with the idea of beauty. From references to beauty in the poems, can you begin to formulate your own account of what beauty actually meant to Hopkins? Discuss with other students how his idea of beauty compares with your own.

4 'Hopkins' fondness for sound effect in his poems is largely bound up with his sensuous feelings for sound.'
'No, it's more to do with his belief that everything in nature is part of a single harmony; sound patterns mirror the patterns he sees in nature.'
What are your own views?

5 In a group, choose two or three poems which employ **sprung rhythm**. Discuss where the stresses should fall, then tape different versions of the poems and compare results. Assess how far this has improved your understanding of Hopkins' use of rhythm.

6 Choose several consecutive stanzas from *The Wreck of the Deutschland*. Using different colours, highlight the different patterns of sound effect you think Hopkins employs. Can you see any links between the meanings in a stanza and the sounds used to express them?

7 How important do you consider sympathy for Hopkins' religious beliefs is when you are responding to his poetry?

8 Hopkins referred to *The Wreck of the Deutschland* as an ode. Look up some definitions of that term, then use anthologies to read some other odes, preferably written before Hopkins' ode, so poems he was likely to have known. The eighteenth-century poets William Cowper and Thomas Gray both wrote famous odes, as did the Romantics John Keats and Percy Bysshe Shelley. In a group discuss how far the subject matter, themes, structure and style of other odes can be helpful when reading *The Wreck of the Deutschland*.

9 You have been asked to choose four or five of the poems in this selection for an anthology with the general theme of nature *or* religion. You have been asked to supply the titles and your reasons for choosing them. In addition, the editor wants you to write a brief introduction for fellow students, intended to highlight important aspects of style and subject matter. Which would you choose? Why? What points would you stress about them?

10 One claim made in the Approaches (p. 138) was that *perfect integration of voice, form and theme happens quite rarely in the poems*. Select one or two of the poems which have made an impression on you, and say how far, if at all, your enjoyment in reading them depends on *integration of voice, form and theme*.

11 *All things counter, original, spare, strange* (7) (*Pied Beauty* p. 19). From your own reading of this selection, how well do you think Hopkins catches the diversity and contrasts of nature in his poems?

12 'Where are the women in these poems? The few who crop up are either virgins or martyrs or both.' Is this fair comment? If it is, would you regard the absence of women from much of the poetry as a deficiency in Hopkins?

13 Choose some poems which take specific people as their initial focus. How far do these poems allow you to reconstruct a sense of the qualities Hopkins found attractive in human nature?

Hopkins the Jesuit priest in 1879: this dates from his time as a parish priest in Oxford and Liverpool. The sonnet, *Felix Randall* (p.29), draws powerfully on his experiences in that vocation

Hopkins' manuscript for *The Windhover* (pp. 18, 67, 102)

Away in the lovable west (*The Wreck of the Deutschland* line 185): this part of Clwyd around St Beuno's College provided the aesthetic inspiration behind such poems as *The Windhover* (p. 18)

It was graphic images such as this of the sinking *Deutschland*, in newspapers of the time, which prompted Hopkins' initial thoughts for his most ambitious poem: *The breakers rolled on her beam with ruinous shock* (line 109, pp. 3–14)

A portrait of the young Robert Bridges, Hopkins' life-long friend and correspondent and first editor. He was also the dedicatee of Hopkins' final sonnet, *To R. B.* (p. 48)

Index of Titles and First Lines